ISBN 0-8373-2138-7

C-2138   CAREER EXAMINATION SERIES

This is your
PASSBOOK® for...

Examiner, Social Services

Test Preparation Study Guide

Questions & Answers

NLC

NATIONAL LEARNING CORPORATION

(516) 921-8888
(800) 645-6337
FAX: (516) 921-8743
www.passbooks.com
sales @ passbooks.com
info @ passbooks.com

PRINTED IN THE UNITED STATES OF AMERICA

PASSBOOK®

NOTICE

PASSBOOK® SERIES

THE *PASSBOOK® SERIES* has been created to prepare applicants and candidates for the ultimate academic battlefield — the examination room.

At some time in our lives, each and every one of us may be required to take an examination — for validation, matriculation, admission, qualification, registration, certification, or licensure.

Based on the assumption that every applicant or candidate has met the basic formal educational standards, has taken the required number of courses, and read the necessary texts, the *PASSBOOK® SERIES* furnishes the one special preparation which may assure passing with confidence, instead of failing with insecurity. Examination questions — together with answers — are furnished as the basic vehicle for study so that the mysteries of the examination and its compounding difficulties may be eliminated or diminished by a sure method.

This book is meant to help you pass your examination provided that you qualify and are serious in your objective.

The entire field is reviewed through the huge store of content information which is succinctly presented through a provocative and challenging approach — the question-and-answer method.

A climate of success is established by furnishing the correct answers at the end of each test.

You soon learn to recognize types of questions, forms of questions, and patterns of questioning. You may even begin to anticipate expected outcomes.

You perceive that many questions are repeated or adapted so that you can gain acute insights, which may enable you to score many sure points.

You learn how to confront new questions, or types of questions, and to attack them confidently and work out the correct answers.

You note objectives and emphases, and recognize pitfalls and dangers, so that you may make positive educational adjustments.

Moreover, you are kept fully informed in relation to new concepts, methods, practices, and directions in the field.

You discover that you are actually taking the examination all the time: you are preparing for the examination by "taking" an examination, not by reading extraneous and/or supererogatory textbooks.

In short, this PASSBOOK®, used directedly, should be an important factor in helping you to pass your test.

EXAMINER, SOCIAL SERVICES

DUTIES AND RESPONSIBILITIES

An employee in this class determines financial eligibility for programs administered by the Department of Social Services, and recommends amounts of assistance in accordance with established policies and procedures. This class is distinguished by the fact that the employee conducts personal interviews with applicants, computes budgets for applicants and determines or reviews applicants' eligibility for assistance. Some workers may be assigned to a unit responsible for performing fieldwork to obtain collateral verification of information to be used in the eligibility determination process. The incumbent works under close supervision at first, but is expected to develop considerable initiative and judgment as experience is gained. Does related work as required.

TESTS

The written test will cover knowledge, skills, and/or abilities in such areas as:

1. Interpreting and applying written material relating to social services programs and/or policies, including using basic arithmetic computations;
2. Understanding and interpreting written material;
3. Preparing written material;
4. Dealing with people in an interviewing situation.

HOW TO TAKE A TEST

I. YOU MUST PASS AN EXAMINATION

A. WHAT EVERY CANDIDATE SHOULD KNOW

Examination applicants often ask us for help in preparing for the written test. What can I study in advance? What kinds of questions will be asked? How will the test be given? How will the papers be graded?

As an applicant for a civil service examination, you may be wondering about some of these things. Our purpose here is to suggest effective methods of advance study and to describe civil service examinations.

Your chances for success on this examination can be increased if you know how to prepare. Those "pre-examination jitters" can be reduced if you know what to expect. You can even experience an adventure in good citizenship if you know why civil service exams are given.

B. WHY ARE CIVIL SERVICE EXAMINATIONS GIVEN?

Civil service examinations are important to you in two ways. As a citizen, you want public jobs filled by employees who know how to do their work. As a job seeker, you want a fair chance to compete for that job on an equal footing with other candidates. The best-known means of accomplishing this two-fold goal is the competitive examination.

Exams are widely publicized throughout the nation. They may be administered for jobs in federal, state, city, municipal, town or village governments or agencies.

Any citizen may apply, with some limitations, such as the age or residence of applicants. Your experience and education may be reviewed to see whether you meet the requirements for the particular examination. When these requirements exist, they are reasonable and applied consistently to all applicants. Thus, a competitive examination may cause you some uneasiness now, but it is your privilege and safeguard.

C. HOW ARE CIVIL SERVICE EXAMS DEVELOPED?

Examinations are carefully written by trained technicians who are specialists in the field known as "psychological measurement," in consultation with recognized authorities in the field of work that the test will cover. These experts recommend the subject matter areas or skills to be tested; only those knowledges or skills important to your success on the job are included. The most reliable books and source materials available are used as references. Together, the experts and technicians judge the difficulty level of the questions.

Test technicians know how to phrase questions so that the problem is clearly stated. Their ethics do not permit "trick" or "catch" questions. Questions may have been tried out on sample groups, or subjected to statistical analysis, to determine their usefulness.

Written tests are often used in combination with performance tests, ratings of training and experience, and oral interviews. All of these measures combine to form the best-known means of finding the right person for the right job.

II. HOW TO PASS THE WRITTEN TEST

A. NATURE OF THE EXAMINATION

To prepare intelligently for civil service examinations, you should know how they differ from school examinations you have taken. In school you were assigned certain definite pages to read or subjects to cover. The examination questions were quite detailed and usually emphasized memory. Civil service exams, on the other hand, try to discover your present ability to perform the duties of a position, plus your potentiality to learn these duties. In other words, a civil service exam attempts to predict how successful you will be. Questions cover such a broad area that they cannot be as minute and detailed as school exam questions.

In the public service similar kinds of work, or positions, are grouped together in one "class." This process is known as *position-classification*. All the positions in a class are paid according to the salary range for that class. One class title covers all of these positions, and they are all tested by the same examination.

B. FOUR BASIC STEPS

1) Study the announcement

How, then, can you know what subjects to study? Our best answer is: "Learn as much as possible about the class of positions for which you've applied." The exam will test the knowledge, skills and abilities needed to do the work.

Your most valuable source of information about the position you want is the official exam announcement. This announcement lists the training and experience qualifications. Check these standards and apply only if you come reasonably close to meeting them.

The brief description of the position in the examination announcement offers some clues to the subjects which will be tested. Think about the job itself. Review the duties in your mind. Can you perform them, or are there some in which you are rusty? Fill in the blank spots in your preparation.

Many jurisdictions preview the written test in the exam announcement by including a section called "Knowledge and Abilities Required," "Scope of the Examination," or some similar heading. Here you will find out specifically what fields will be tested.

2) Review your own background

Once you learn in general what the position is all about, and what you need to know to do the work, ask yourself which subjects you already know fairly well and which need improvement. You may wonder whether to concentrate on improving your strong areas or on building some background in your fields of weakness. When the announcement has specified "some knowledge" or "considerable knowledge," or has used adjectives like "beginning principles of..." or "advanced ... methods," you can get a clue as to the number and difficulty of questions to be asked in any given field. More questions, and hence broader coverage, would be included for those subjects which are more important in the work. Now weigh your strengths and weaknesses against the job requirements and prepare accordingly.

3) Determine the level of the position

Another way to tell how intensively you should prepare is to understand the level of the job for which you are applying. Is it the entering level? In other words, is this the position in which beginners in a field of work are hired? Or is it an intermediate or advanced level? Sometimes this is indicated by such words as "Junior" or "Senior" in the class title. Other jurisdictions use Roman numerals to designate the level – Clerk I, Clerk II, for example. The word "Supervisor" sometimes appears in the title. If the level is not indicated by the title, check the description of duties. Will you be working under very close supervision, or will you have responsibility for independent decisions in this work?

4) Choose appropriate study materials

Now that you know the subjects to be examined and the relative amount of each subject to be covered, you can choose suitable study materials. For beginning level jobs, or even advanced ones, if you have a pronounced weakness in some aspect of your training, read a modern, standard textbook in that field. Be sure it is up to date and has general coverage. Such books are normally available at your library, and the librarian will be glad to help you locate one. For entry-level positions, questions of appropriate difficulty are chosen – neither highly advanced questions, nor those too simple. Such questions require careful thought but not advanced training.

If the position for which you are applying is technical or advanced, you will read more advanced, specialized material. If you are already familiar with the basic principles of your field, elementary textbooks would waste your time. Concentrate on advanced textbooks and technical periodicals. Think through the concepts and review difficult problems in your field.

These are all general sources. You can get more ideas on your own initiative, following these leads. For example, training manuals and publications of the government agency which employs workers in your field can be useful, particularly for technical and professional positions. A letter or visit to the government department involved may result in more specific study suggestions, and certainly will provide you with a more definite idea of the exact nature of the position you are seeking.

III. KINDS OF TESTS

Tests are used for purposes other than measuring knowledge and ability to perform specified duties. For some positions, it is equally important to test ability to make adjustments to new situations or to profit from training. In others, basic mental abilities not dependent on information are essential. Questions which test these things may not appear as pertinent to the duties of the position as those which test for knowledge and information. Yet they are often highly important parts of a fair examination. For very general questions, it is almost impossible to help you direct your study efforts. What we can do is to point out some of the more common of these general abilities needed in public service positions and describe some typical questions.

1) General information

Broad, general information has been found useful for predicting job success in some kinds of work. This is tested in a variety of ways, from vocabulary lists to questions about current events. Basic background in some field of work, such as sociology or economics, may be sampled in a group of questions. Often these are principles which have become familiar to most persons through exposure rather than through formal training. It is difficult to advise you how to study for these questions; being alert to the world around you is our best suggestion.

2) Verbal ability

An example of an ability needed in many positions is verbal or language ability. Verbal ability is, in brief, the ability to use and understand words. Vocabulary and grammar tests are typical measures of this ability. Reading comprehension or paragraph interpretation questions are common in many kinds of civil service tests. You are given a paragraph of written material and asked to find its central meaning.

3) Numerical ability

Number skills can be tested by the familiar arithmetic problem, by checking paired lists of numbers to see which are alike and which are different, or by interpreting charts and graphs. In the latter test, a graph may be printed in the test booklet which you are asked to use as the basis for answering questions.

4) Observation

A popular test for law-enforcement positions is the observation test. A picture is shown to you for several minutes, then taken away. Questions about the picture test your ability to observe both details and larger elements.

5) Following directions

In many positions in the public service, the employee must be able to carry out written instructions dependably and accurately. You may be given a chart with several columns, each column listing a variety of information. The questions require you to carry out directions involving the information given in the chart.

6) Skills and aptitudes

Performance tests effectively measure some manual skills and aptitudes. When the skill is one in which you are trained, such as typing or shorthand, you can practice. These tests are often very much like those given in business school or high school courses. For many of the other skills and aptitudes, however, no short-time preparation can be made. Skills and abilities natural to you or that you have developed throughout your lifetime are being tested.

Many of the general questions just described provide all the data needed to answer the questions and ask you to use your reasoning ability to find the answers. Your best preparation for these tests, as well as for tests of facts and ideas, is to be at your physical and mental best. You, no doubt, have your own methods of getting into an exam-taking mood and keeping "in shape." The next section lists some ideas on this subject.

IV. KINDS OF QUESTIONS

Only rarely is the "essay" question, which you answer in narrative form, used in civil service tests. Civil service tests are usually of the short-answer type. Full instructions for answering these questions will be given to you at the examination. But in case this is your first experience with short-answer questions and separate answer sheets, here is what you need to know:

1) Multiple-choice Questions

Most popular of the short-answer questions is the "multiple choice" or "best answer" question. It can be used, for example, to test for factual knowledge, ability to solve problems or judgment in meeting situations found at work.

A multiple-choice question is normally one of three types—
- It can begin with an incomplete statement followed by several possible endings. You are to find the one ending which *best* completes the statement, although some of the others may not be entirely wrong.
- It can also be a complete statement in the form of a question which is answered by choosing one of the statements listed.

- It can be in the form of a problem – again you select the best answer.

Here is an example of a multiple-choice question with a discussion which should give you some clues as to the method for choosing the right answer:

When an employee has a complaint about his assignment, the action which will *best* help him overcome his difficulty is to
- A. discuss his difficulty with his coworkers
- B. take the problem to the head of the organization
- C. take the problem to the person who gave him the assignment
- D. say nothing to anyone about his complaint

In answering this question, you should study each of the choices to find which is best. Consider choice "A" – Certainly an employee may discuss his complaint with fellow employees, but no change or improvement can result, and the complaint remains unresolved. Choice "B" is a poor choice since the head of the organization probably does not know what assignment you have been given, and taking your problem to him is known as "going over the head" of the supervisor. The supervisor, or person who made the assignment, is the person who can clarify it or correct any injustice. Choice "C" is, therefore, correct. To say nothing, as in choice "D," is unwise. Supervisors have and interest in knowing the problems employees are facing, and the employee is seeking a solution to his problem.

2) True/False Questions

The "true/false" or "right/wrong" form of question is sometimes used. Here a complete statement is given. Your job is to decide whether the statement is right or wrong.

SAMPLE: A roaming cell-phone call to a nearby city costs less than a non-roaming call to a distant city.

This statement is wrong, or false, since roaming calls are more expensive.

This is not a complete list of all possible question forms, although most of the others are variations of these common types. You will always get complete directions for answering questions. Be sure you understand *how* to mark your answers – ask questions until you do.

V. RECORDING YOUR ANSWERS

Computer terminals are used more and more today for many different kinds of exams.

For an examination with very few applicants, you may be told to record your answers in the test booklet itself. Separate answer sheets are much more common. If this separate answer sheet is to be scored by machine – and this is often the case – it is highly important that you mark your answers correctly in order to get credit.

An electronic scoring machine is often used in civil service offices because of the speed with which papers can be scored. Machine-scored answer sheets must be marked with a pencil, which will be given to you. This pencil has a high graphite content which responds to the electronic scoring machine. As a matter of fact, stray dots may register as answers, so do not let your pencil rest on the answer sheet while you are pondering the correct answer. Also, if your pencil lead breaks or is otherwise defective, ask for another.

Since the answer sheet will be dropped in a slot in the scoring machine, be careful not to bend the corners or get the paper crumpled.

The answer sheet normally has five vertical columns of numbers, with 30 numbers to a column. These numbers correspond to the question numbers in your test booklet. After each number, going across the page are four or five pairs of dotted lines. These short dotted lines have small letters or numbers above them. The first two pairs may also have a "T" or "F" above the letters. This indicates that the first two pairs only are to be used if the questions are of the true-false type. If the questions are multiple choice, disregard the "T" and "F" and pay attention only to the small letters or numbers.

Answer your questions in the manner of the sample that follows:

32. The largest city in the United States is
    A. Washington, D.C.
    B. New York City
    C. Chicago
    D. Detroit
    E. San Francisco

1) Choose the answer you think is best. (New York City is the largest, so "B" is correct.)
2) Find the row of dotted lines numbered the same as the question you are answering. (Find row number 32)
3) Find the pair of dotted lines corresponding to the answer. (Find the pair of lines under the mark "B.")
4) Make a solid black mark between the dotted lines.

VI. BEFORE THE TEST

Common sense will help you find procedures to follow to get ready for an examination. Too many of us, however, overlook these sensible measures. Indeed, nervousness and fatigue have been found to be the most serious reasons why applicants fail to do their best on civil service tests. Here is a list of reminders:

- Begin your preparation early – Don't wait until the last minute to go scurrying around for books and materials or to find out what the position is all about.
- Prepare continuously – An hour a night for a week is better than an all-night cram session. This has been definitely established. What is more, a night a week for a month will return better dividends than crowding your study into a shorter period of time.
- Locate the place of the exam – You have been sent a notice telling you when and where to report for the examination. If the location is in a different town or otherwise unfamiliar to you, it would be well to inquire the best route and learn something about the building.
- Relax the night before the test – Allow your mind to rest. Do not study at all that night. Plan some mild recreation or diversion; then go to bed early and get a good night's sleep.
- Get up early enough to make a leisurely trip to the place for the test – This way unforeseen events, traffic snarls, unfamiliar buildings, etc. will not upset you.
- Dress comfortably – A written test is not a fashion show. You will be known by number and not by name, so wear something comfortable.

- Leave excess paraphernalia at home – Shopping bags and odd bundles will get in your way. You need bring only the items mentioned in the official notice you received; usually everything you need is provided. Do not bring reference books to the exam. They will only confuse those last minutes and be taken away from you when in the test room.
- Arrive somewhat ahead of time – If because of transportation schedules you must get there very early, bring a newspaper or magazine to take your mind off yourself while waiting.
- Locate the examination room – When you have found the proper room, you will be directed to the seat or part of the room where you will sit. Sometimes you are given a sheet of instructions to read while you are waiting. Do not fill out any forms until you are told to do so; just read them and be prepared.
- Relax and prepare to listen to the instructions
- If you have any physical problem that may keep you from doing your best, be sure to tell the test administrator. If you are sick or in poor health, you really cannot do your best on the exam. You can come back and take the test some other time.

VII. AT THE TEST

The day of the test is here and you have the test booklet in your hand. The temptation to get going is very strong. Caution! There is more to success than knowing the right answers. You must know how to identify your papers and understand variations in the type of short-answer question used in this particular examination. Follow these suggestions for maximum results from your efforts:

1) Cooperate with the monitor

The test administrator has a duty to create a situation in which you can be as much at ease as possible. He will give instructions, tell you when to begin, check to see that you are marking your answer sheet correctly, and so on. He is not there to guard you, although he will see that your competitors do not take unfair advantage. He wants to help you do your best.

2) Listen to all instructions

Don't jump the gun! Wait until you understand all directions. In most civil service tests you get more time than you need to answer the questions. So don't be in a hurry. Read each word of instructions until you clearly understand the meaning. Study the examples, listen to all announcements and follow directions. Ask questions if you do not understand what to do.

3) Identify your papers

Civil service exams are usually identified by number only. You will be assigned a number; you must not put your name on your test papers. Be sure to copy your number correctly. Since more than one exam may be given, copy your exact examination title.

4) Plan your time

Unless you are told that a test is a "speed" or "rate of work" test, speed itself is usually not important. Time enough to answer all the questions will be provided, but this does not mean that you have all day. An overall time limit has been set. Divide the total time (in minutes) by the number of questions to determine the approximate time you have for each question.

5) Do not linger over difficult questions

If you come across a difficult question, mark it with a paper clip (useful to have along) and come back to it when you have been through the booklet. One caution if you do this – be sure to skip a number on your answer sheet as well. Check often to be sure that you have not lost your place and that you are marking in the row numbered the same as the question you are answering.

6) Read the questions

Be sure you know what the question asks! Many capable people are unsuccessful because they failed to *read* the questions correctly.

7) Answer all questions

Unless you have been instructed that a penalty will be deducted for incorrect answers, it is better to guess than to omit a question.

8) Speed tests

It is often better NOT to guess on speed tests. It has been found that on timed tests people are tempted to spend the last few seconds before time is called in marking answers at random – without even reading them – in the hope of picking up a few extra points. To discourage this practice, the instructions may warn you that your score will be "corrected" for guessing. That is, a penalty will be applied. The incorrect answers will be deducted from the correct ones, or some other penalty formula will be used.

9) Review your answers

If you finish before time is called, go back to the questions you guessed or omitted to give them further thought. Review other answers if you have time.

10) Return your test materials

If you are ready to leave before others have finished or time is called, take ALL your materials to the monitor and leave quietly. Never take any test material with you. The monitor can discover whose papers are not complete, and taking a test booklet may be grounds for disqualification.

VIII. EXAMINATION TECHNIQUES

1) Read the general instructions carefully. These are usually printed on the first page of the exam booklet. As a rule, these instructions refer to the timing of the examination; the fact that you should not start work until the signal and must stop work at a signal, etc. If there are any *special* instructions, such as a choice of questions to be answered, make sure that you note this instruction carefully.

2) When you are ready to start work on the examination, that is as soon as the signal has been given, read the instructions to each question booklet, underline any key words or phrases, such as *least, best, outline, describe* and the like. In this way you will tend to answer as requested rather than discover on reviewing your paper that you *listed without describing*, that you selected the *worst* choice rather than the *best* choice, etc.

3) If the examination is of the objective or multiple-choice type – that is, each question will also give a series of possible answers: A, B, C or D, and you are called upon to select the best answer and write the letter next to that answer on your answer paper – it is advisable to start answering each question in turn. There may be anywhere from 50 to 100 such questions in the three or four hours allotted and you can see how much time would be taken if you read through all the questions before beginning to answer any. Furthermore, if you come across a question or group of questions which you know would be difficult to answer, it would undoubtedly affect your handling of all the other questions.

4) If the examination is of the essay type and contains but a few questions, it is a moot point as to whether you should read all the questions before starting to answer any one. Of course, if you are given a choice – say five out of seven and the like – then it is essential to read all the questions so you can eliminate the two that are most difficult. If, however, you are asked to answer all the questions, there may be danger in trying to answer the easiest one first because you may find that you will spend too much time on it. The best technique is to answer the first question, then proceed to the second, etc.

5) Time your answers. Before the exam begins, write down the time it started, then add the time allowed for the examination and write down the time it must be completed, then divide the time available somewhat as follows:
   - If 3-1/2 hours are allowed, that would be 210 minutes. If you have 80 objective-type questions, that would be an average of 2-1/2 minutes per question. Allow yourself no more than 2 minutes per question, or a total of 160 minutes, which will permit about 50 minutes to review.
   - If for the time allotment of 210 minutes there are 7 essay questions to answer, that would average about 30 minutes a question. Give yourself only 25 minutes per question so that you have about 35 minutes to review.

6) The most important instruction is to *read each question* and make sure you know what is wanted. The second most important instruction is to *time yourself properly* so that you answer every question. The third most important instruction is to *answer every question*. Guess if you have to but include something for each question. Remember that you will receive no credit for a blank and will probably receive some credit if you write something in answer to an essay question. If you guess a letter – say "B" for a multiple-choice question – you may have guessed right. If you leave a blank as an answer to a multiple-choice question, the examiners may respect your feelings but it will not add a point to your score. Some exams may penalize you for wrong answers, so in such cases *only*, you may not want to guess unless you have some basis for your answer.

7) Suggestions
   a. Objective-type questions
      1. Examine the question booklet for proper sequence of pages and questions
      2. Read all instructions carefully
      3. Skip any question which seems too difficult; return to it after all other questions have been answered
      4. Apportion your time properly; do not spend too much time on any single question or group of questions

5. Note and underline key words – *all, most, fewest, least, best, worst, same, opposite,* etc.
6. Pay particular attention to negatives
7. Note unusual option, e.g., unduly long, short, complex, different or similar in content to the body of the question
8. Observe the use of "hedging" words – *probably, may, most likely,* etc.
9. Make sure that your answer is put next to the same number as the question
10. Do not second-guess unless you have good reason to believe the second answer is definitely more correct
11. Cross out original answer if you decide another answer is more accurate; do not erase until you are ready to hand your paper in
12. Answer all questions; guess unless instructed otherwise
13. Leave time for review

b. Essay questions
1. Read each question carefully
2. Determine exactly what is wanted. Underline key words or phrases.
3. Decide on outline or paragraph answer
4. Include many different points and elements unless asked to develop any one or two points or elements
5. Show impartiality by giving pros and cons unless directed to select one side only
6. Make and write down any assumptions you find necessary to answer the questions
7. Watch your English, grammar, punctuation and choice of words
8. Time your answers; don't crowd material

8) Answering the essay question

Most essay questions can be answered by framing the specific response around several key words or ideas. Here are a few such key words or ideas:

M's: manpower, materials, methods, money, management
P's: purpose, program, policy, plan, procedure, practice, problems, pitfalls, personnel, public relations
   a. Six basic steps in handling problems:
   1. Preliminary plan and background development
   2. Collect information, data and facts
   3. Analyze and interpret information, data and facts
   4. Analyze and develop solutions as well as make recommendations
   5. Prepare report and sell recommendations
   6. Install recommendations and follow up effectiveness

   b. Pitfalls to avoid
   1. *Taking things for granted* – A statement of the situation does not necessarily imply that each of the elements is necessarily true; for example, a complaint may be invalid and biased so that all that can be taken for granted is that a complaint has been registered

2. *Considering only one side of a situation* – Wherever possible, indicate several alternatives and then point out the reasons you selected the best one
3. *Failing to indicate follow up* – Whenever your answer indicates action on your part, make certain that you will take proper follow-up action to see how successful your recommendations, procedures or actions turn out to be
4. *Taking too long in answering any single question* – Remember to time your answers properly

IX. AFTER THE TEST

Scoring procedures differ in detail among civil service jurisdictions although the general principles are the same. Whether the papers are hand-scored or graded by machine we have described, they are nearly always graded by number. That is, the person who marks the paper knows only the number – never the name – of the applicant. Not until all the papers have been graded will they be matched with names. If other tests, such as training and experience or oral interview ratings have been given, scores will be combined. Different parts of the examination usually have different weights. For example, the written test might count 60 percent of the final grade, and a rating of training and experience 40 percent. In many jurisdictions, veterans will have a certain number of points added to their grades.

After the final grade has been determined, the names are placed in grade order and an eligible list is established. There are various methods for resolving ties between those who get the same final grade – probably the most common is to place first the name of the person whose application was received first. Job offers are made from the eligible list in the order the names appear on it. You will be notified of your grade and your rank as soon as all these computations have been made. This will be done as rapidly as possible.

People who are found to meet the requirements in the announcement are called "eligibles." Their names are put on a list of eligible candidates. An eligible's chances of getting a job depend on how high he stands on this list and how fast agencies are filling jobs from the list.

When a job is to be filled from a list of eligibles, the agency asks for the names of people on the list of eligibles for that job. When the civil service commission receives this request, it sends to the agency the names of the three people highest on this list. Or, if the job to be filled has specialized requirements, the office sends the agency the names of the top three persons who meet these requirements from the general list.

The appointing officer makes a choice from among the three people whose names were sent to him. If the selected person accepts the appointment, the names of the others are put back on the list to be considered for future openings.

That is the rule in hiring from all kinds of eligible lists, whether they are for typist, carpenter, chemist, or something else. For every vacancy, the appointing officer has his choice of any one of the top three eligibles on the list. This explains why the person whose name is on top of the list sometimes does not get an appointment when some of the persons lower on the list do. If the appointing officer chooses the second or third eligible, the No. 1 eligible does not get a job at once, but stays on the list until he is appointed or the list is terminated.

X. HOW TO PASS THE INTERVIEW TEST

The examination for which you applied requires an oral interview test. You have already taken the written test and you are now being called for the interview test – the final part of the formal examination.

You may think that it is not possible to prepare for an interview test and that there are no procedures to follow during an interview. Our purpose is to point out some things you can do in advance that will help you and some good rules to follow and pitfalls to avoid while you are being interviewed.

What is an interview supposed to test?

The written examination is designed to test the technical knowledge and competence of the candidate; the oral is designed to evaluate intangible qualities, not readily measured otherwise, and to establish a list showing the relative fitness of each candidate – as measured against his competitors – for the position sought. Scoring is not on the basis of "right" and "wrong," but on a sliding scale of values ranging from "not passable" to "outstanding." As a matter of fact, it is possible to achieve a relatively low score without a single "incorrect" answer because of evident weakness in the qualities being measured.

Occasionally, an examination may consist entirely of an oral test – either an individual or a group oral. In such cases, information is sought concerning the technical knowledges and abilities of the candidate, since there has been no written examination for this purpose. More commonly, however, an oral test is used to supplement a written examination.

Who conducts interviews?

The composition of oral boards varies among different jurisdictions. In nearly all, a representative of the personnel department serves as chairman. One of the members of the board may be a representative of the department in which the candidate would work. In some cases, "outside experts" are used, and, frequently, a businessman or some other representative of the general public is asked to serve. Labor and management or other special groups may be represented. The aim is to secure the services of experts in the appropriate field.

However the board is composed, it is a good idea (and not at all improper or unethical) to ascertain in advance of the interview who the members are and what groups they represent. When you are introduced to them, you will have some idea of their backgrounds and interests, and at least you will not stutter and stammer over their names.

What should be done before the interview?

While knowledge about the board members is useful and takes some of the surprise element out of the interview, there is other preparation which is more substantive. It *is* possible to prepare for an oral interview – in several ways:

1) Keep a copy of your application and review it carefully before the interview

This may be the only document before the oral board, and the starting point of the interview. Know what education and experience you have listed there, and the sequence and dates of all of it. Sometimes the board will ask you to review the highlights of your experience for them; you should not have to hem and haw doing it.

2) Study the class specification and the examination announcement

Usually, the oral board has one or both of these to guide them. The qualities, characteristics or knowledges required by the position sought are stated in these documents. They offer valuable clues as to the nature of the oral interview. For example, if the job involves supervisory responsibilities, the announcement will usually indicate that knowledge of modern supervisory methods and the qualifications of the candidate as a supervisor will be tested. If so, you can expect such questions, frequently in the form of a hypothetical situation which you are expected to solve. NEVER go into an oral without knowledge of the duties and responsibilities of the job you seek.

3) Think through each qualification required

Try to visualize the kind of questions you would ask if you were a board member. How well could you answer them? Try especially to appraise your own knowledge and background in each area, *measured against the job sought*, and identify any areas in which you are weak. Be critical and realistic – do not flatter yourself.

4) Do some general reading in areas in which you feel you may be weak

For example, if the job involves supervision and your past experience has NOT, some general reading in supervisory methods and practices, particularly in the field of human relations, might be useful. Do NOT study agency procedures or detailed manuals. The oral board will be testing your understanding and capacity, not your memory.

5) Get a good night's sleep and watch your general health and mental attitude

You will want a clear head at the interview. Take care of a cold or any other minor ailment, and of course, no hangovers.

What should be done on the day of the interview?

Now comes the day of the interview itself. Give yourself plenty of time to get there. Plan to arrive somewhat ahead of the scheduled time, particularly if your appointment is in the fore part of the day. If a previous candidate fails to appear, the board might be ready for you a bit early. By early afternoon an oral board is almost invariably behind schedule if there are many candidates, and you may have to wait. Take along a book or magazine to read, or your application to review, but leave any extraneous material in the waiting room when you go in for your interview. In any event, relax and compose yourself.

The matter of dress is important. The board is forming impressions about you – from your experience, your manners, your attitude, and your appearance. Give your personal appearance careful attention. Dress your best, but not your flashiest. Choose conservative, appropriate clothing, and be sure it is immaculate. This is a business interview, and your appearance should indicate that you regard it as such. Besides, being well groomed and properly dressed will help boost your confidence.

Sooner or later, someone will call your name and escort you into the interview room. *This is it.* From here on you are on your own. It is too late for any more preparation. But remember, you asked for this opportunity to prove your fitness, and you are here because your request was granted.

What happens when you go in?

The usual sequence of events will be as follows: The clerk (who is often the board stenographer) will introduce you to the chairman of the oral board, who will introduce you to the other members of the board. Acknowledge the introductions before you sit down. Do not be surprised if you find a microphone facing you or a stenotypist sitting by. Oral interviews are usually recorded in the event of an appeal or other review.

Usually the chairman of the board will open the interview by reviewing the highlights of your education and work experience from your application – primarily for the benefit of the other members of the board, as well as to get the material into the record. Do not interrupt or comment unless there is an error or significant misinterpretation; if that is the case, do not hesitate. But do not quibble about insignificant matters. Also, he will usually ask you some question about your education, experience or your present job – partly to get you to start talking and to establish the interviewing "rapport." He may start the actual questioning, or turn it over to one of the other members. Frequently, each member undertakes the questioning on a particular area, one in which he is perhaps most competent, so you can expect each member to participate in the examination. Because time is limited, you may also expect some rather abrupt switches in the direction the questioning takes, so do not be upset by it. Normally, a board member will not pursue a single line of questioning unless he discovers a particular strength or weakness.

After each member has participated, the chairman will usually ask whether any member has any further questions, then will ask you if you have anything you wish to add. Unless you are expecting this question, it may floor you. Worse, it may start you off on an extended, extemporaneous speech. The board is not usually seeking more information. The question is principally to offer you a last opportunity to present further qualifications or to indicate that you have nothing to add. So, if you feel that a significant qualification or characteristic has been overlooked, it is proper to point it out in a sentence or so. Do not compliment the board on the thoroughness of their examination – they have been sketchy, and you know it. If you wish, merely say, "No thank you, I have nothing further to add." This is a point where you can "talk yourself out" of a good impression or fail to present an important bit of information. Remember, *you close the interview yourself.*

The chairman will then say, "That is all, Mr. _____, thank you." Do not be startled; the interview is over, and quicker than you think. Thank him, gather your belongings and take your leave. Save your sigh of relief for the other side of the door.

How to put your best foot forward

Throughout this entire process, you may feel that the board individually and collectively is trying to pierce your defenses, seek out your hidden weaknesses and embarrass and confuse you. Actually, this is not true. They are obliged to make an appraisal of your qualifications for the job you are seeking, and they want to see you in your best light. Remember, they must interview all candidates and a non-cooperative candidate may become a failure in spite of their best efforts to bring out his qualifications. Here are 15 suggestions that will help you:

1) Be natural – Keep your attitude confident, not cocky

If you are not confident that you can do the job, do not expect the board to be. Do not apologize for your weaknesses, try to bring out your strong points. The board is interested in a positive, not negative, presentation. Cockiness will antagonize any board member and make him wonder if you are covering up a weakness by a false show of strength.

2) Get comfortable, but don't lounge or sprawl

Sit erectly but not stiffly. A careless posture may lead the board to conclude that you are careless in other things, or at least that you are not impressed by the importance of the occasion. Either conclusion is natural, even if incorrect. Do not fuss with your clothing, a pencil or an ashtray. Your hands may occasionally be useful to emphasize a point; do not let them become a point of distraction.

3) Do not wisecrack or make small talk

This is a serious situation, and your attitude should show that you consider it as such. Further, the time of the board is limited – they do not want to waste it, and neither should you.

4) Do not exaggerate your experience or abilities

In the first place, from information in the application or other interviews and sources, the board may know more about you than you think. Secondly, you probably will not get away with it. An experienced board is rather adept at spotting such a situation, so do not take the chance.

5) If you know a board member, do not make a point of it, yet do not hide it

Certainly you are not fooling him, and probably not the other members of the board. Do not try to take advantage of your acquaintanceship – it will probably do you little good.

6) Do not dominate the interview

Let the board do that. They will give you the clues – do not assume that you have to do all the talking. Realize that the board has a number of questions to ask you, and do not try to take up all the interview time by showing off your extensive knowledge of the answer to the first one.

7) Be attentive

You only have 20 minutes or so, and you should keep your attention at its sharpest throughout. When a member is addressing a problem or question to you, give him your undivided attention. Address your reply principally to him, but do not exclude the other board members.

8) Do not interrupt

A board member may be stating a problem for you to analyze. He will ask you a question when the time comes. Let him state the problem, and wait for the question.

9) Make sure you understand the question

Do not try to answer until you are sure what the question is. If it is not clear, restate it in your own words or ask the board member to clarify it for you. However, do not haggle about minor elements.

10) Reply promptly but not hastily

A common entry on oral board rating sheets is "candidate responded readily," or "candidate hesitated in replies." Respond as promptly and quickly as you can, but do not jump to a hasty, ill-considered answer.

11) Do not be peremptory in your answers

A brief answer is proper – but do not fire your answer back. That is a losing game from your point of view. The board member can probably ask questions much faster than you can answer them.

12) Do not try to create the answer you think the board member wants

He is interested in what kind of mind you have and how it works – not in playing games. Furthermore, he can usually spot this practice and will actually grade you down on it.

13) Do not switch sides in your reply merely to agree with a board member

Frequently, a member will take a contrary position merely to draw you out and to see if you are willing and able to defend your point of view. Do not start a debate, yet do not surrender a good position. If a position is worth taking, it is worth defending.

14) Do not be afraid to admit an error in judgment if you are shown to be wrong

The board knows that you are forced to reply without any opportunity for careful consideration. Your answer may be demonstrably wrong. If so, admit it and get on with the interview.

15) Do not dwell at length on your present job

The opening question may relate to your present assignment. Answer the question but do not go into an extended discussion. You are being examined for a *new* job, not your present one. As a matter of fact, try to phrase ALL your answers in terms of the job for which you are being examined.

Basis of Rating

Probably you will forget most of these "do's" and "don'ts" when you walk into the oral interview room. Even remembering them all will not ensure you a passing grade. Perhaps you did not have the qualifications in the first place. But remembering them will help you to put your best foot forward, without treading on the toes of the board members.

Rumor and popular opinion to the contrary notwithstanding, an oral board wants you to make the best appearance possible. They know you are under pressure – but they also want to see how you respond to it as a guide to what your reaction would be under the pressures of the job you seek. They will be influenced by the degree of poise you display, the personal traits you show and the manner in which you respond.

ABOUT THIS BOOK

This book contains tests divided into Examination Sections. Go through each test, answering every question in the margin. We have also attached a sample answer sheet at the back of the book that can be removed and used. At the end of each test look at the answer key and check your answers. On the ones you got wrong, look at the right answer choice and learn. Do not fill in the answers first. Do not memorize the questions and answers, but understand the answer and principles involved. On your test, the questions will likely be different from the samples. Questions are changed and new ones added. If you understand these past questions you should have success with any changes that arise. Tests may consist of several types of questions. We have additional books on each subject should more study be advisable or necessary for you. Finally, the more you study, the better prepared you will be. This book is intended to be the last thing you study before you walk into the examination room. Prior study of relevant texts is also recommended. NLC publishes some of these in our Fundamental Series. Knowledge and good sense are important factors in passing your exam. Good luck also helps. So now study this Passbook, absorb the material contained within and take that knowledge into the examination. Then do your best to pass that exam.

––––––––

EXAMINATION SECTION

EXAMINATION SECTION
TEST 1

DIRECTIONS: Each question or incomplete statement is followed by several suggested answers or completions. Select the one that BEST answers the question or completes the statement. *PRINT THE LETTER OF THE CORRECT ANSWER IN THE SPACE AT THE RIGHT.*

1. You find that an applicant for public assistance is hesitant about showing you some required personal material and documents. Your INITIAL reaction to this situation should be to

    A. quietly insist that he give you the required materials
    B. make an exception in his case to avoid making him uncomfortable
    C. suspect that he may be trying to withhold evidence
    D. understand that he is in a stressful situation and may feel ashamed to reveal such information

1.____

2. An applicant has just given you a response which does not seem clear. Of the following. the BEST course of action for you to take in order to check your understanding of the applicant's response is for you to

    A. ask the question again during a subsequent interview with this applicant
    B. repeat the applicant's answer in the applicant.s own words and ask if that is what the applicant meant
    C. later in the interview, repeat the question that led to this response
    D. repeat the question that led to this response, but say it more forcefully

2.____

3. While speaking with applicants for public assistance, you may find that there are times when an applicant will be silent for a short while before answering questions. In order to gather the BEST information from the applicant, the interviewer should *generally* treat these silences by

    A. repeating the same question to make the applicant stop hesitating
    B. rephrasing the question in a way that the applicant can answer it faster
    C. directing an easier question to the applicant so that he can gain confidence in answering
    D. waiting patiently and not pressuring the applicant into quick undeveloped answers

3.____

4. In dealing with members of different ethnic and religious groups among the applicants you interview, you should give

    A. individuals the services to which they are entitled
    B. less service to those you judge to be more advantaged
    C. better service to groups with which you sympathize most
    D. better service to group with political *muscle*

4.____

5. You must be sure that, when interviewing an applicant, you phrase each question carefully. Of the following, the MOST important reason for this is to insure that

    A. the applicant will phrase each of his responses carefully
    B. you use correct grammar
    C. it is clear to the applicant what information you are seeking
    D. you do not word the same question differently for different applicants

5.____

6. When given a form to complete, a client hesitates, tells you that he cannot fill out forms too well, and that he is afraid he will do a poor job. He asks you to do it for him. You are quite sure, however, that he is able to do it himself. In this case, it would be MOST advisable for you to

    A. encourage him to try filling out the application as well as he can
    B. fill out the application for him
    C. explain to him that he must learn to accept responsibility
    D. tell him that, if others can fill out an application, he can too

7. Assume that an applicant for public assistance whom you are interviewing has made a statement that is obviously not true. Of the following, the BEST course of action for you to take at this point in the interview is to

    A. ask the applicant if he is sure about his statement
    B. tell the applicant that his statement is incorrect
    C. question the applicant further to clarify his response
    D. assume that the statement is true

8. Assume that you are conducting an initial interview with an applicant for public assistance. Of the following, the MOST advisable questions for you to ask at the beginning of this interview are questions that

    A. can be answered in one or two sentences
    B. have nothing to do with the subject matter of the interview
    C. are most likely to reveal any hostility on the part of the applicant
    D. the applicant is most likely to be willing and able to answer

9. When interviewing a particularly nervous and upset applicant for public assistance, the one of the following actions which you should take FIRST is to

    A. inform the applicant that, to be helped, he must cooperate
    B. advise the applicant that proof must be provided for statements he makes
    C. assure the applicant that every effort will be made to provide him with whatever assistance he is entitled to
    D. tell the applicant he will have no trouble obtaining public assistance so long as he is truthful

10. Assume that, following normal routine, it is part of your job to prepare a monthly report for your unit head that eventually goes to the Director of your Center. The report contains information on the number of applicants you have interviewed that have been approved for different types of public assistance and the number of applicants you have interviewed that have been turned down. Errors on such reports are *serious* because

    A. you are expected to be able to prove how many applicants you have interviewed each month
    B. accurate statistics are needed for effective management of the department
    C. they may not be discovered before the report is transmitted to the Center Director
    D. they may result in a loss of assistance to the applicants left out of the report

11. During interviews, people give information about themselves in several ways. Which of the following *usually* gives the LEAST amount of information about the person being questioned? His

    A. spoken words   B. tone of voice
    C. facial expression   D. body position

11.____

12. Suppose an applicant, while being interviewed about his eligibility for public assistance, becomes angered by your questioning and begins to use sharp, uncontrolled language. Which of the following is the BEST way for you to react to him?

    A. Speak in his style to show him that you are neither impressed nor upset by his speech
    B. Interrupt him and tell him that you are not required to listen to this kind of speech
    C. Lower your voice and slow the rate of your speech in an attempt to set an example that will calm him
    D. Let him continue in his way but insist that he answer your questions directly

12.____

13. You have been informed that no determination has yet been made on the eligibility of an applicant for public assistance. The decision depends on further checking. His situation, however, is similar to that of many other applicants whose eligibility has been approved. The applicant calls you, quite worried, and asks you whether his application has been accepted. What would be BEST for you to do under these circumstances? Tell him

    A. his application is being checked and you will let him know the final result as soon as possible
    B. that a written request addressed to your supervisor will probably get faster action for his case
    C. not to worry since other applicants with similar backgrounds have already been accepted
    D. since there is no definite information and you are very busy, you will call him back

13.____

14. Suppose that you have been talking with an applicant for public assistance. You have the feeling from the latest things the applicant has said that some of his answers to earlier questions were not totally correct. You guess that he might have been afraid or confused earlier but that your conversation has now put him in a more comfortable frame of mind. In order to test the reliability of information received from the earlier questions, the BEST thing for you to do *now* is to ask new questions that

    A. allow the applicant to explain why he deliberately gave false information to you
    B. ask for the same information, although worded differently from the original questions
    C. put pressure on the applicant so that he personally wants to clear up the facts in his earlier answers
    D. indicate to the applicant that you are aware of his deceptiveness

14.____

15. Assume that you are a supervisor. While providing you with required information, an applicant for public assistance informs you that she does not know who is the father of her child. Of the following, the MOST advisable action for you to take is to

    A. ask her to explain further
    B. advise her about birth control facilities
    C. express your sympathy for the situation
    D. go on to the next item of information

15.____

16. If, in an interview, you wish to determine a client.s usual occupation, which one of the fol- 16.____
lowing questions is MOST likely to elicit the most useful information?

    A. Did you ever work in a factory?
    B. Do you know how to do office work?
    C. What kind of work do you do?
    D. Where are you working now?

17. Assume that, in the course of the day, you are approached by a clerk from another office 17.____
who starts questioning you about one of the clients you have just interviewed. The clerk
says that she is a relative of the client. According to departmental policy, all matters discussed with clients are to be kept confidential. Of the following, the BEST course of
action for you to take in this situation would be to

    A. check to see whether the clerk is really a relative before you make any further deci-
sion
    B. explain to the clerk why you cannot divulge the information
    C. tell the clerk that you do not know the answers to her questions
    D. tell the clerk that she can get from the client any information the client wishes to
give

18. Which of the following is *usually* the BEST technique for you, as an interviewer, to use to 18.____
bring an applicant back to subject matter from which the applicant has strayed?

    A. Ask the applicant a question that is related to the subject of the interview
    B. Show the applicant that his response is unrelated to the question
    C. Discreetly remind the applicant that there is a time allotment for the interview
    D. Tell the applicant that you will be happy to discuss the extraneous matters at a
future interview

19. Assume that you notice that one of the clerks has accidentally pulled the wrong form to 19.____
give to her client. Of the following, the BEST way for you to handle this situation would be
to tell

    A. the clerk about her error, and precisely describe the problems that will result
    B. the clerk about her error in an understanding and friendly way
    C. the clerk about her error in a humorous way and tell her that no real damage was
done
    D. your supervisor that clerks need more training in the use and application of depart-
mental forms

20. Of the following characteristics, the one which would be MOST valuable when helping an 20.____
angry applicant to understand why he has received less assistance than he believes he
is entitled to would be the ability to

    A. state the rules exactly as they apply to the applicant's problem
    B. cite examples of other cases where the results have been similar
    C. remain patient and understanding of the person's feelings
    D. remain completely objective and uninvolved in individual personal problems

21. Reports are usually divided into several sections, some of which are more necessary   21.____
    than others. Of the following, the section which is MOST often necessary to include in a
    report is a(n)

    A. table of contents   B. introduction
    C. index   D. bibliography

22. Suppose you are writing a report on an interview you have just completed with a particu-   22.____
    larly hostile applicant for public assistance. Which of the following BEST describes what
    you should include in this report?

    A. What you think caused the applicant.s hostile attitude during the interview
    B. Specific examples of the applicant.s hostile remarks and behavior
    C. The relevant information uncovered during the interview
    D. A recommendation that the applicant.s request be denied because of his hostility

23. When including recommendations in a report to your supervisor, which of the following is   23.____
    MOST important for you to do?

    A. Provide several alternative courses of action for each recommendation
    B. First present the supporting evidence, then the recommendations
    C. First present the recommendations, then the supporting evidence
    D. Make sure the recommendations arise logically out of the information in the report

24. It is often necessary that the writer of a report present facts and sufficient arguments to   24.____
    gain acceptance of the points, conclusions, or recommendations set forth in the report.
    Of the following, the LEAST advisable step to take in organizing a report, when such
    argumentation is the important factor, is a(n)

    A. elaborate expression of personal belief
    B. businesslike discussion of the problem as a whole
    C. orderly arrangement of convincing data
    D. reasonable explanation of the primary issues

25. Suppose you receive a phone call from an applicant about a problem which requires that   25.____
    you must look up the information and call her back. Although the applicant had given you
    her name earlier and you can pronounce the name, you are not sure that you can spell it
    correctly. Asking the applicant to spell her name is

    A. *good,* because this indicates to the applicant that you intend to obtain the informa-
tion she requested
    B. *poor,* because she may feel you are making fun of her name
    C. *good,* because you will be sure to get the correct name
    D. *poor,* because she will think you have not been listening to her

KEY (CORRECT ANSWERS)

1.	D		11.	D
2.	B		12.	C
3.	D		13.	A
4.	A		14.	B
5.	C		15.	D
6.	A		16.	C
7.	C		17.	B
8.	D		18.	A
9.	C		19.	B
10.	B		20.	C

21.	B
22.	C
23.	D
24.	A
25.	C

TEST 2

DIRECTIONS: Each question or incomplete statement is followed by several suggested answers or completions. Select the one that BEST answers the question or completes the statement. *PRINT THE LETTER OF THE CORRECT ANSWER IN THE SPACE AT THE RIGHT.*

Questions 1-9.

DIRECTIONS: Answer Questions 1 through 9 SOLELY on the basis of the information in the following passage.

The establishment of a procedure whereby the client's rent is paid directly by the Social Service agency has been suggested recently by many people in the Social Service field. It is believed that such a procedure would be advantageous to both the agency and the client. Under the current system, clients often complain that their rent allowances are not for the correct amount. Agencies, in turn, have had to cope with irate landlords who complain that they are not receiving rent checks until much later than their due date.

The proposed new system would involve direct payment of the client's rent by the agency to the landlord. Clients would not receive a monthly rent allowance. Under one possible implementation of such a system, special rent payment offices would be set up in each borough and staffed by Social Service clerical personnel. Each office would handle all work involved in sending out monthly rent payments. Each client would receive monthly notification from the Social Service agency that his rent has been paid. A rent office would be established for every three Social Service centers in each borough. Only in cases where the rental exceeds $700 per month would payment be made and records kept by the Social Service center itself rather than a special rent office. However, clients would continue to make all direct contacts through the Social Service center.

Files in the rent offices would be organized on the basis of client rental. All cases involving monthly rents up to, but not exceeding, $300 would be placed in salmon-colored folders. Cases with rents from $301 to $500 would be placed in buff folders, and those with rents exceeding $500, but less than $700 would be filed in blue folders. If a client's rental changed, he would be required to notify the center as soon as possible so that this information could be brought up-to-date in his folder, and the color of his folder changed if necessary. Included in the information needed, in addition to the amount of rent, are the size of the apartment, the type of heat, and the number of flights of stairs to climb if there is no elevator.

Discussion as to whether the same information should be required of clients residing in city projects was resolved with the decision that the identical system of filing and updating of files should apply to such project tenants. The basic problem that might arise from the institution of such a program is that clients would resent being unable to pay their own rent. However, it is likely that such resentment would be only a temporary reaction to change and would disappear after the new system became standard procedure. It has been suggested that this program first be experimented with on a small scale to determine what problems may arise and how the program can be best implemented.

1. According to the passage, there are a number of complaints about the current system of rent payments. Which of the following is a *complaint* expressed in the passage?   1.____

   A. Landlords complain that clients sometimes pay the wrong amount for their rent.
   B. Landlords complain that clients sometimes do not pay their rent on time.

C. Clients say that the Social Service agency sometimes does not mail the rent out on time.

D. Landlords say that they sometimes fail to receive a check for the rent.

2. Assume that there are 15 Social Service centers in Manhattan. According to the passage, the number of rent offices that should be established in that borough under the new system is

   A. 1   B. 3   C. 5   D. 15

2.____

3. According to the passage, a client under the new system would receive

   A. a rent receipt from the landlord indicating that Social Services has paid the rent
   B. nothing since his rent has been paid by Social Services
   C. verification from the landlord that the rent was paid
   D. notices of rent payment from the Social Service agency

3.____

4. According to the passage, a case record involving a client whose rent has changed from $310 to $540 per month should be changed from a ____ folder to a ____ folder.

   A. blue; salmon-colored   B. buff; blue
   C. salmon-colored; blue   D. yellow; buff

4.____

5. According to the above passage, if a client's rental is lowered because of violations in his building, he would be required to notify the

   A. building department   B. landlord
   C. rent payment office   D. Social Service center

5.____

6. Which one of the following kinds of information about a rented apartment is NOT mentioned in the above passage as being necessary to include in the client's folder? The

   A. floor number, if in an apartment house with an elevator
   B. rental, if in a city project apartment
   C. size of the apartment, if in a two-family house
   D. type of heat, if in a city project apartment

6.____

7. Assume that the rent payment proposal discussed in the passage is approved and ready for implementation in the city. Which of the following actions is MOST in accordance with the proposal described in the above passage?

   A. Change over completely and quickly to the new system to avoid the confusion of having clients under both systems.
   B. Establish rent payment offices in all of the existing Social Service centers.
   C. Establish one small rent payment office in Manhattan for about six months.
   D. Set up an office in each borough and discontinue issuing rent allowances.

7.____

8. According to the passage, it can be *inferred* that the MOST important drawback of the new system would be that once a program is started, clients might feel

   A. they have less independence than they had before
   B. unable to cope with problems that mature people should be able to handle
   C. too far removed from Social Service personnel to successfully adapt to the new requirements
   D. too independent to work with the system

8.____

9. The above passage suggests that the proposed rent program be started as a pilot pro-   9._____
gram rather than be instituted immediately throughout the city. Of the following possible
reasons for a pilot program, the one which is stated in the passage as the MOST direct
reason is that

    A. any change made would then be only on a temporary basis
    B. difficulties should be determined from small-scale implementation
    C. implementation on a wide scale is extremely difficult
    D. many clients might resent the new system

10. A report is often revised several times before final preparation and distribution in an effort   10._____
to make certain the report meets the needs of the situation for which it is designed.
Which of the following is the BEST way for the author to be sure that a report covers the
areas he intended?

    A. Obtain a co-worker's opinion.
    B. Compare it with a content checklist.
    C. Test it on a subordinate.
    D. Check his bibliography.

11. Visual aids used in a report may be placed either in the text material or in the appendix.   11._____
Deciding where to put a chart, table, or any such aid should depend on the

    A. title of the report   B. purpose of the visual aid
    C. title of the visual aid   D. length of the report

12. In which of the following situations is an oral report PREFERABLE to a written report?   12._____
When a(n)

    A. recommendation is being made for a future plan of action
    B. department head requests immediate information
    C. long standing policy change is made
    D. analysis of complicated statistical data is involved

13. When an applicant is approved for public assistance, standard forms with certain infor-   13._____
mation must be filled in.
The GREATEST advantage of using standard forms in this situation rather than writing
the report as you see fit is that

    A. the report can be acted on quickly
    B. the report can be written without directions from a supervisor
    C. needed information is less likely to be left out of the report
    D. information that is written up this way is more likely to be verified

14. In some types of reports, visual aids add interest, meaning, and support. They also pro-   14._____
vide an essential means of effectively communicating the message of the report.
Of the following, the selection of the suitable visual aids to use with a report is LEAST
dependent on the

    A. nature and scope of the report   B. way in which the aid is to be used
    C. aids used in other reports   D. prospective readers of the report

15. He wanted to ASCERTAIN the facts before arriving at a conclusion. The word ASCER-   15.___
    TAIN means *most nearly*

    A. disprove   B. determine   C. convert   D. provide

16. Did the supervisor ASSENT to her request for annual leave? The word ASSENT means   16.___
    most nearly

    A. allude   B. protest   C. agree   D. refer

17. The new worker was fearful that the others would REBUFF her. The word REBUFF   17.___
    means *most nearly*

    A. ignore   B. forget   C. copy   D. snub

18. The supervisor of that office does not CONDONE lateness. The word CONDONE means   18.___
    most nearly

    A. mind   B. excuse   C. punish   D. remember

19. Each employee was instructed to be as CONCISE as possible when preparing a report.   19.___
    The word CONCISE means *most nearly*

    A. exact   B. sincere   C. flexible   D. brief

20. Despite many requests for them, there was a SCANT supply of new blotters. The word   20.___
    SCANT means *most nearly*

    A. adequate   B. abundant
    C. insufficient   D. expensive

21. Did they REPLENISH the supply of forms in the cabinet? The word REPLENISH means   21.___
    most nearly

    A. straighten up   B. refill
    C. sort out   D. use

22. Employees may become bored if they are assigned DIVERSE duties. The word   22.___
    DIVERSE means *most nearly*

    A. interesting   B. different
    C. challenging   D. enjoyable

23. During the probation period, the worker proved to be INEPT. The word INEPT means   23.___
    most nearly

    A. incompetent   B. insubordinate
    C. satisfactory   D. uncooperative

24. The PUTATIVE father was not living with the family. The word PUTATIVE means *most*   24.___
    nearly

    A. reputed   B. unemployed
    C. concerned   D. indifferent

25. The adopted child researched various documents of VITAL STATISTICS in an effort to   25.___
    discover the names of his natural parents. The words VITAL STATISTICS means *most*
    nearly statistics relating to

    A. human life   B. hospitals
    C. important facts   D. health and welfare

KEY (CORRECT ANSWERS)

1.	B	11.	B
2.	C	12.	B
3.	D	13.	C
4.	B	14.	C
5.	D	15.	B
6.	A	16.	C
7.	C	17.	D
8.	A	18.	B
9.	B	19.	D
10.	B	20.	C

21.	B
22.	B
23.	A
24.	A
25.	A

———

EXAMINATION SECTION
TEST 1

DIRECTIONS: Each question or incomplete statement is followed by several suggested answers or completions. Select the one that BEST answers the question or completes the statement. *PRINT THE LETTER OF THE CORRECT ANSWER IN THE SPACE AT THE RIGHT.*

Questions 1-4.

DIRECTIONS: Questions 1 through 4 are to be answered SOLELY on the basis of the information in the paragraphs below.

Some authorities have questioned whether the term "culture of poverty" should be used since "culture" means a design for living which is passed down from generation to generation. The culture of poverty is, however, a very useful concept if it is used with care, with recognition that poverty is a subculture, and with avoidance of the "cookie-cutter" approach. With regard to the individual, the cookie-cutter view assumes that all individuals in a culture turn out exactly alike, as if they were so many cookies. It overlooks the fact that, at least in our urban society, every individual is a member of more than one subculture; and which subculture most strongly influences his response in a given situation depends on the interaction of a great many factors, including his individual makeup and history, the specifics of the various subcultures to which he belongs, and the specifics of the given situation. It is always important to avoid the cookie-cutter view of culture, with regard to the individual and to the culture or subculture involved.

With regard to the culture as a whole, the cookie-cutter concept again assumes homogeneity and consistency. It forgets that within any one culture or subculture there are conflicts and contradictions, and that at any given moment an individual may have to choose, consciously, between conflicting values or patterns. Also, most individuals, in varying degrees, have a dual set of values - those by which they live and those they cherish as best. This point has been made and documented repeatedly about the culture of poverty.

1.   The *cookie-cutter* approach assumes that   1._____

      A.   members of the same *culture* are all alike
      B.   *culture* stays the same from generation to generation
      C.   the term *culture* should not be applied to groups who are poor
      D.   there are value conflicts within most cultures

2.   According to the passage, every person in our cities   2._____

      A.   is involved in the conflicts of urban culture
      B.   recognizes that poverty is a subculture
      C.   lives by those values to which he is exposed
      D.   belongs to more than one subculture

3.   The above passage emphasizes that a culture is likely to contain within it   3._____

      A.   one dominant set of values
      B.   a number of contradictions

    C.   one subculture to which everyone belongs
    D.   members who are exactly alike

4.   According to the above passage, individuals are sometimes forced to choose between   4._____

    A.   cultures
    B.   subcultures
    C.   different sets of values
    D.   a new culture and an old culture

Questions 5-8.

DIRECTIONS: Questions 5 through 8 are to be answered SOLELY on the basis of the follow-
                 ing passage.

*There are approximately 33 million poor people in the United States; 14.3 million of them
are children, 5.3 million are old people, and the remainder are in other categories. Altogether,
6.5 million families live in poverty because the heads of the households cannot works they
are either too old or too sick or too severely handicapped, or they are widowed or deserted
mothers of young children. There are the working poor, the low-paid workers, the workers in
seasonal industries, and soldiers with no additional income who are heads of families. There
are the underemployed: those who would like full-time jobs but cannot find them, those
employees who would like year-round work but lack the opportunity, and those who are
employed below their level of training. There are the non-working poor: the older men and
women With small retirement incomes and those with no income, the disabled, the physically
and mentally handicapped, and the chronically sick.*

5.   According to the above passage, APPROXIMATELY what percent of the poor people in   5._____
    the United States are children?

    A. 33   B. 16   C. 20   D. 44

6.   According to the above passage, people who work in seasonal industries are LIKELY to   6._____
    be classified as

    A.   working poor   B.   underemployed
    C.   non-working poor   D.   low-paid workers

7.   According to the above passage, the category of non-working poor includes people who   7._____

    A.   receive unemployment insurance
    B.   cannot find full-time work
    C.   are disabled or mentally handicapped
    D.   are soldiers with wives and children

8.   According to the above passage, among the underemployed are those who   8._____

    A.   can find only part-time work
    B.   are looking for their first jobs
    C.   are inadequately trained
    D.   depend on insufficient retirement incomes

Questions 9-18.

DIRECTIONS: Questions 9 through 18 are to be answered SOLELY on the basis of the information given in the following charts.

CHILD CARE SERVICES 1997-2001

CHILDREN IN FOSTER HOMES AND VOLUNTARY INSTITUTIONS, BY TYPE OF CARE, IN NEW YORK CITY AND UPSTATE* NEW YORK

| Year End | FOSTER FAMILY HOMES | | | Total in Foster Family Homes | Total in Voluntary Institutions | Total in Other | Total Number of Children |
	Boarding Homes	Adoptive or Free Homes	Wage, Work or Self-Supportine				
New York City							
1997	12,389	1,773	33	14,195	7,187	1,128	22,510
1998	13,271	1,953	42	15,266	7,227	1,237	23,730
1999	14,012	2,134	32	16,178	7,087	1,372	24,637
2000	14,558	2,137	29	16,724	6,717	1,437	24,778
2001	14,759	2,241	37	17,037	6,777	1,455	25,264
Up-state							
1997	14,801	2,902	90	17,793	3,012	241	21,046
1998	15,227	2,943	175	18,345	3,067	291	21,703
1999	16,042	3,261	64	19,367	2,940	273	22,580
2000	16,166	3,445	60	19,671	2,986	362	23,121
2001	16,357	3,606	55	20,018	3.024	485	23,527

*Upstate is defined as all of New York State, excluding New York City.

NUMBER OF CHILDREN, BY AGE, UNDER FOSTER FAMILY CARE IN NEW YORK CITY IN 2001

| Borough | Children's Ages | | | | | Total All Ages |
	One Year or Younger	Two Years	Three Years	Four Years	Over Four Years	
Manhattan	1,054	1,170	1,060	1,325	445	5,070
Bronx	842	1,196	1,156	1,220	484	4,882
Brooklyn	707	935	470	970	361	?
Queens	460	555	305	793	305	2,418
Richmond	270	505	160	173	112	1.224
Total All Boroughs	3,337	4,361	3,151	4,481	?	17,037

9. According to the table, Child Care Services, 1997-2001, the number of children in New York City boarding homes was AT LEAST twice the number of children in New York City voluntary institutions in _____ of the five years.

    A. *only* one   B. *only* two   C. *only* three   D. all

9.____

10. If the number of children cared for in voluntary institutions in New York State increases from 2001 to 2002 by exactly the same number as from 2000 to 2001, then the 2002 year-end total of children in voluntary institutions in New York State will be

    A. 3,062   B. 6,837   C. 7,494   D. 9,899

10.____

11. If the total number of children under child care services in New York City in 1997 was 25% more than in 1996, then the 1996 New York City total was MOST NEARLY

    A. 11,356   B. 11,647   C. 16,883   D. 18,008

11.____

12. From 1997 through 2001, the New York State five-year average of children in Child Care Services classified as *other* is MOST NEARLY

    A. 330   B. 728   C. 1,326   D. 1,656

12.____

13. Of all the children under foster family care in the Bronx in 2001, the percentage who were one year of age or younger is MOST NEARLY

    A. 16%   B. 17%   C. 18%   D. 19%

13.____

14. Suppose that in New York State the *wage, work, or self-supporting* type of foster family care is given only to children between the ages of 14 and 18, and that, of the children in *adoptive or free home* foster care in each of the five years listed, only one percent each year are between the ages of 14 and 18.
The TOTAL number of 14 to 18-year-olds under foster family care in Upstate New York exceeded 95 in _____ of the five years.

    A. each   B. four   C. three   D. two

14.____

15. The average number of two-year-olds under foster family care in New York City's boroughs in 2001 is MOST NEARLY

    A. 872   B. 874   C. 875   D. 882

15.____

16. The difference between the total number of children of all ages under foster family care in Brooklyn in 2001 and the total number under foster care in Richmond that year is

    A. 1,224   B. 2,219   C. 3,443   D. 4,667

16.____

17. Suppose that by the end of 2002 the number of children one year or younger under foster family care in Queens will be twice the 2001 total, while the number of two-year-olds will be four-fifths the 2001 total.
The 2002 total of children two years or younger under foster family care in Queens will be

    A. 2,418   B. 1,624   C. 1,364   D. 1,015

17.____

18. The TOTAL number oi children over four years of age under foster care in New York City in 2001 was

    A. 1,607   B. 1,697   C. 1,707   D. 1,797

18.____

19. At the start of a year, a family was receiving a public assistance grant of $191 twice a   19.____
month, on the 1st and 15th of each month. On March 1, their rent allowance was
decreased from $75 to $71 a month since they had moved to a smaller apartment. On
August 1, their semimonthly food allowance, which had been $40.20, was raised by 10%.
In that year, the TOTAL amount of money disbursed to this family was

    A. $2,272.10   B. $3,290.70
    C. $4,544.20   D. $4,584.20

20. It is discovered that a client has received double public assistance for 2 months by having   20.____
been enrolled at two service centers of the Department of Social Services. The client
should have received $84.00 twice a month instead of the double amount. He now
agrees to repay the money by equal deductions from his public assistance check over a
period of 12 months.
What will the amount of his NEXT check be?

    A. $56   B. $70   C. $77   D. $80

21. Suppose a study is being made of the composition of 3,550 families receiving public   21.____
assistance. Of the first 1,050 families reviewed, 18% had four or more children.
If, in the remaining number of families, the percentage with four or more children is half
as high as the percentage in the group already reviewed, then the percentage of families with four or more children in the entire group of families is MOST NEARLY

    A. 12   B. 14   C. 16   D. 27

22. Suppose that food prices have risen 13%, and an increase of the same amount has been   22.____
granted in the food allotment given to people receiving public assistance.
If a family has been receiving $405 a month, 35% of which is allotted for food, then the
TOTAL amount of public assistance this family receives per month will be changed to

    A. $402.71   B. $420.03   C. $423.43   D. $449.71

23. Assume that the food allowance is to be raised 5% in August but will be retroactive for   23.____
four months to April. The retroactive allowance is to be divided into equal sections and
added to the public assistance checks for August, September, October, November, and
December.
A family which has been receiving $420 monthly, 40% of which was allotted for food,
will receive what size check in August?

    A. $426.72   B. $428.40   C. $430.50   D. $435.12

24. A blind client, who receives $105 public assistance twice a month, inherits 14 shares of   24.____
stock worth $90 each. The client is required to sell the stock and spend his inheritance
before receiving more public assistance.
Using his public assistance allowance as a guide, how many months are his new
assets expected to last?

    A. 6   B. 7   C. 8   D. 12

25. The Department of Social Services has 16 service centers in Manhattan. These centers   25.____
     may be divided into those which are downtown (south of Central Park) and those which
     are uptown. Two of the centers are special service centers and are downtown, while the
     remainder of the centers are general service centers. There is a total of 7 service centers
     downtown.
     The percentage of the general service centers which are uptown is MOST NEARLY

     A. 56   B. 64   C. 69   D. 79

KEY (CORRECT ANSWERS)

1.	A		11.	D
2.	D		12.	D
3.	B		13.	B
4.	C		14.	C
5.	D		15.	A
6.	A		16.	B
7.	C		17.	C
8.	A		18.	C
9.	B		19.	D
10.	D		20.	B

21.	A
22.	C
23.	D
24.	A
25.	B

TEST 2

DIRECTIONS: Each question or incomplete statement is followed by several suggested answers or completions. Select the one that BEST answers the question or completes the statement. *PRINT THE LETTER OF THE CORRECT ANSWER IN THE SPACE AT THE RIGHT.*

1. On January 1, a family was receiving supplementary monthly public assistance of $56 for food, $48 for rent, and $28 for other necessities. In the spring, their rent rose by 10%, and their rent allowance was adjusted accordingly.
   In the summer, due to the death of a family member, their allotments for food and other necessities were reduced by 1/7.
   Their monthly allowance check in the fall should be   1.____

   A. $124.80   B. $128.80   C. $132.80   D. $136.80

2. Twice a month, a certain family receives a $170 general allowance for rent, food, and clothing expenses. In addition, the family receives a specific supplementary allotment for utilities of $192 a year, which is added to their semi-monthly check.
   If the general allowance alone is reduced by 5%, what will be the TOTAL amount of their next semi-monthly check?   2.____

   A. $161.50   B. $169.50   C. $170.00   D. $177.50

3. If each clerk in a certain unit sees an average of 9 clients in a 7-hour day and there are 15 clerks in the unit, APPROXIMATELY how many clients will be seen in a 35-hour week?   3.____

   A. 315   B. 405   C. 675   D. 945

4. The program providing federal welfare aid to the state and its cities is intended to expand services to public assistance recipients.
   All of the following services are included in the program EXCEPT   4.____

   A. homemaker/housekeeper services
   B. mental health clinics
   C. abortion clinics
   D. narcotic addiction control services

5. The Department of Consumer Affairs is NOT concerned with regulation of   5.____

   A. prices   B. product service guarantees
   C. welfare fraud   D. product misrepresentation

6. A plan to control the loss of welfare monies would likely contain all of the following EXCEPT   6.____

   A. identification cards with photographs of the welfare client
   B. individual cash payments to each member of a family
   C. computerized processing of welfare money records
   D. face-to-face interviews with the welfare clients

7. The state law currently allows a woman to obtain an abortion 7.____

    A. only if it is intended to save her life
    B. if three doctors confirm the need for such treatment
    C. if it does not conflict with her religious beliefs
    D. upon her request, up to the 24th week of pregnancy

8. Under the city's public assistance program, allocations for payment of a client's rent and 8.____
security deposits are given in check form directly to the welfare recipient and not to the
landlord.
This practice is used in the city MAINLY as an effort to

    A. increase the client's responsibility for his own affairs
    B. curb the rent overcharges made by most landlords in the city
    C. control the number of welfare recipients housed in public housing projects
    D. limit the number of checks issued to each welfare family

9. The city plans to save 100 million dollars a year in public assistance costs. 9.____
To achieve this goal, the Human Resources Administration and the Department of
Social Services may take any of the following steps EXCEPT

    A. tightening controls on public assistance eligibility requirements
    B. intensifying the investigations of relief frauds
    C. freezing the salaries of all agency employees for a one-year period
    D. cutting the services extended to public assistance clients

10. Recently, the state instituted a work relief program under which employable recipients of 10.____
Home Relief and Aid to Dependent Children are given jobs to help work off their relief
grants.
Under the present work relief program, program recipients are NOT required to

    A. report to state employment offices every two weeks to pick up their welfare checks
    B. live within a two-mile radius of the job site to which they are referred
    C. respond to offers of part-time jobs in public agencies
    D. take job training courses offered through the State Employment Service

11. Of the following, the MOST inclusive program designed to help selected cities to sub- 11.____
stantially improve social, physical, and economic conditions in specially selected slum
neighborhoods is known as the

    A. Model Cities Program
    B. Neighborhood Youth Corps Program
    C. Urban Renewal Program
    D. Emergency Employment Act

12. The crusade against environmental hazards in the United States is concentrated in 12.____
urban areas MOSTLY on the problems of

    A. air pollution, sewage treatment, and noise
    B. garbage collection
    C. automobile exhaust fumes and street cleanliness
    D. recycling, reconstitution, and open space

Questions 13-16.

DIRECTIONS: Questions 13 through 16 are to be answered SOLELY on the basis of the information in the following passage.

City social work agencies and the police have been meeting at City Hall to coordinate efforts to defuse the tensions among teenage groups that they fear could flare into warfare once summer vacations begin. Police intelligence units, with the help of the District Attorneys' offices, are gathering information to identify gangs and their territories. A list of 3, 000 gang members has already been assembled, and 110 gangs have been identified. Social workers from various agencies like the Department of Social Services, Neighborhood youth Corps, and the Youth Board are out every day developing liaison with groups of juveniles through meetings at schools and recreation centers. Many street workers spend their days seeking to ease the intergang hostility, tracing potentially incendiary rumors, and trying to channel willing gang members into participation in established summer programs. The city's Youth Services Agency plans to spend a million dollars for special summer programs in ten main city areas where gang activity is most firmly entrenched. Five of the "gang neighborhoods" are clustered in an area forming most of southeastern Bronx, and it is here that most of the 110 identified gangs have formed. Special Youth Services programs will also be directed toward the Rockaway section of Queens, Chinatown, Washington Heights, and two neighborhoods in northern Staten Island noted for a lot of motorcycle gang activity. Some of these programs will emphasize sports and recreation, others vocational guidance or neighborhood improvement, but each program will be aimed at benefiting all youngsters in the area. Although none of the money will be spent specifically on gang members, the Youth Services Agency is consulting gang leaders, along with other teenagers, on the projects they would like developed in their area.

13. The above passage states that one of the steps taken by street workers in trying to defuse the tensions among teenage gangs is that of   13._____

    A. conducting summer school sessions that will benefit all neighborhood youth
    B. monitoring neighborhood sports competitions between rival gangs
    C. developing liaison with community school boards and parent associations
    D. tracing rumors that could intensify intergang hostilities

14. Based on the information given in the above passage on gangs and New York City's gang members, it is CORRECT to state that   14._____

    A. there are no teenage gangs located in Brooklyn
    B. most of the gangs identified by the police are concentrated in one borough
    C. there is a total of 110 gangs in New York City
    D. only a small percentage of gangs in New York City is in Queens

15. According to the above passage, one IMPORTANT aspect of the program is that   15._____

    A. youth gang leaders and other teenagers are involved in the planning
    B. money will be given directly to gang members for use on their projects
    C. only gang members will be allowed to participate in the programs
    D. the parents of gang members will act as youth leaders

16. Various city agencies are cooperating in the attempt to keep the city's youth *cool* during the summer school vacation period.
The above passage does NOT specifically indicate participation in this project by the

    A. Police Department
    B. District Attorney's Office
    C. Board of Education
    D. Department of Social Services

16.____

Questions 17-19.

DIRECTIONS: Questions 17 through 19 are to be answered SOLELY on the basis of the information in the following passage.

It is important that interviewers understand to some degree the manner in which stereotyped thinking operates. Stereotypes are commonly held, but predominantly false, preconceptions about the appearance and traits of individuals of different racial, religious, ethnic, and subcultural groups. Distinct traits, physical and mental, are associated with each group, and membership in a particular group is enough, in the mind of a person holding the stereotype, to assure that these traits will be perceived in individuals who are members of that group. Conversely, possession of the particular stereotyped trait by an individual usually indicates to the holder of the stereotype that the individual is a group member. Linked to the formation of stereotypes is the fact that mental traits, either positive or negative, such as honesty , laziness, avariciousness, and other characteristics are associated with particular stereotypes. Either kind of stereotype, if held by an interviewer, can seriously damage the results of an interview. In general, stereotypes can be particularly dangerous when they are part of the belief patterns of administrators, interviewers, and supervisors, who are in a position to affect the lives of others and to stimulate or retard the development of human potential. The holding of a stereotype by an interviewer, for example, diverts his attention from significant essential facts and information upon which really valid assessments may be made. Unfortunately, it is the rare interviewer who is completely conscious of the real basis upon which he is making his evaluation of the people he is interviewing. The specific reasons given by an interviewer for a negative evaluation, even though apparently logical and based upon what, in the mind of the interviewer, are very good reasons, may not be the truly motivating factors. This is why the careful selection and training of interviewers is such an important responsibility of an agency which is attempting to help a great diversity of human beings.

17. Of the following, the BEST title for the above paragraph is

    A. POSITIVE AND NEGATIVE EFFECTS OF STEREOTYPED THINKING
    B. THE RELATIONSHIP OF STEREOTYPES TO INTERVIEWING
    C. AN AGENCY'S RESPONSIBILITY IN INTERVIEWING
    D. THE IMPACT OF STEREOTYPED THINKING ON PROFESSIONAL FUNCTIONS

17.____

18. According to the above passage, MOST interviewers

    A. compensate for stereotyped beliefs to avoid negatively affecting the results of their interviews
    B. are influenced by stereotypes they hold, but put greater stress on factual information developed during the interview
    C. are seldom aware of their real motives when evaluating interviewees
    D. give logical and good reasons for negative evaluations of interviewees

18.____

19. According to the above passage, which of the following is NOT a characteristic of stereo-   19.____
types?

    A. Stereotypes influence estimates of personality traits of people.
    B. Positive stereotypes can damage the results of an interview.
    C. Physical traits associated with stereotypes seldom really exist.
    D. Stereotypes sometimes are a basis upon which valid personality assessments can
        be made.

Questions 20-25.

DIRECTIONS: Questions 20 through 25 are to be answered SOLELY on the basis of the information in the following passage.

The quality of the voice of a worker is an important factor in conveying to clients and co-workers his attitude and, to some degree, his character. The human voice, when not consciously disguised, may reflect a person's mood, temper, and personality. It has been shown in several experiments that certain character traits can be assessed with better than chance accuracy through listening to the voice of an unknown person who cannot be seen.

Since one of the objectives of the worker is to put clients at ease and to present an encouraging and comfortable atmosphere, a harsh, shrill, or loud voice could have a negative effect. A client who displays emotions of anger or resentment would probably be provoked even further by a caustic tone. In a face-to-face situation, an unpleasant voice may be compensated for to some degree by a concerned and kind facial expression. However, when one speaks on the telephone, the expression on one's face cannot be seen by the listener. A supervising clerk who wishes to represent himself effectively to clients should try to eliminate as many faults as possible in striving to develop desirable voice qualities.

20. If a worker uses a sarcastic tone while interviewing a resentful client, the client, accord-   20.____
ing to the above passage, would MOST likely

    A. avoid the face-to-face situation
    B. be ashamed of his behavior
    C. become more resentful
    D. be provoked to violence

21. According to the above passage, experiments comparing voice and character traits have   21.____
demonstrated that

    A. prospects for improving an unpleasant voice through training are better than
        chance
    B. the voice can be altered to project many different psychological characteristics
    C. the quality of the human voice reveals more about the speaker than his words do
    D. the speaker's voice tells the hearer something about the speaker's personality

22. Which of the following, according to the above passage, is a person's voice MOST likely   22.____
to reveal?
His

    A. prejudices   B. intelligence
    C. social awareness   D. temperament

23. It may be MOST reasonably concluded from the above passage that an interested and sympathetic expression on the face of a worker

    A. may induce a client to feel certain he will receive welfare benefits
    B. will eliminate the need for pleasant vocal qualities in the interviewer
    C. may help to make up for an unpleasant voice in the interviewer
    D. is desirable as the interviewer speaks on the telephone to a client

23.____

24. Of the following, the MOST reasonable implication of the above paragraph is that a worker should, when speaking to a client, control and use his voice to

    A. simulate a feeling of interest in the problems of the client
    B. express his emotions directly and adequately
    C. help produce in the client a sense of comfort and security
    D. reflect his own true personality

24.____

25. It may be concluded from the passage that the PARTICULAR reason for a worker to pay special attention to modulating her voice when talking on the phone to a client is that, during a telephone conversation,

    A. there is a necessity to compensate for the way in which a telephone distorts the voice
    B. the voice of the worker is a reflection of her mood and character
    C. the client can react only on the basis of the voice and words she hears
    D. the client may have difficulty getting a clear understanding over the telephone

25.____

KEY (CORRECT ANSWERS)

1.	A		11.	A
2.	B		12.	A
3.	C		13.	D
4.	C		14.	B
5.	C		15.	A
6.	B		16.	C
7.	D		17.	B
8.	A		18.	C
9.	C		19.	D
10.	B		20.	C

21.	D
22.	D
23.	C
24.	C
25.	C

EXAMINATION SECTION
TEST 1

DIRECTIONS: Each question or incomplete statement is followed by several suggested answers or completions. Select the one that BEST answers the question or completes the statement. *PRINT THE LETTER OF THE CORRECT ANSWER IN THE SPACE AT THE RIGHT.*

1. Assume that an applicant, obviously under a great deal of stress, talks continuously and rambles, making it difficult for you to determine the exact problem and her need. In order to make the interview more successful, it would be BEST for you to
   A. interrupt the applicant and ask her specific questions in order to get the information you need
   B. tell the applicant that her rambling may be a basic cause of her problem
   C. let the applicant continue talking as long as she wishes
   D. ask the applicant to get to the point because other people are waiting for you

1.____

2. A worker must be able to interview clients all day and still be able to listen and maintain interest.
   Of the following, it is MOST important for you to show interest in the client because, if you appear interested,
   A. the client is more likely to appreciate your professional status
   B. the client is more likely to disclose a greater amount of information
   C. the client is less likely to tell lies
   D. you are more likely to gain your supervisor's approval

2.____

3. The application process is overwhelming to applicant Ms. M. She is very anxious and is fearful that she does not have all that she needs to be eligible for assistance. As a result, every time she is asked to produce a verifying document during the interview, she fumbles and drops all the other documents to the floor.
   Of the following, the MOST effective method for you to use to complete the application process is to
   A. ask Ms. M not to be so nervous because you cannot get the work done if she fusses so much
   B. take the documents away from Ms. M and do it your self
   C. suggest that Ms. M get a friend to come and help her with the papers
   D. try to calm Ms. M and tell her that you are willing to help her with the papers to get the information you require

3.____

4. An applicant for public assistance claims that her husband deserted the family and that she needs money immediately for food since her children have not eaten for two days. Under normal procedure, she has to wait several days before she can be given any money for this purpose. In accordance with departmental policy, no exception can be made in this case.
Of the following, the BEST action for you to take is to
    A. tell her that, according to departmental policy, she cannot be given money immediately
    B. purchase some food for her, using your own funds, so that she can feed her children
    C. take up a collection among co-workers
    D. send her to another center

4.____

5. Applicants for public assistance often complain about the length of the application form. They also claim that the questions are too personal, since all they want is money. It is true that the form is long, but the answers to all the questions on the form are needed so that the department can make a decision on eligibility.
When applicants complain, which of the following would be the MOST appropriate action for you to take?
    A. Help such applicants understand that each question has a purpose which will help in the determination of eligibility
    B. Tell such applicants that you agree but that you must comply with regulations because it is your job
    C. Tell such applicants that they should stop complaining if they want you to help
    D. Refer such applicants to a supervisor who will explain agency policy

5.____

6. Which one of the following statements BEST describes the primary goal of a worker?
    A. Process as many clients in as short a time as possible
    B. Help his clients
    C. Grow into a more understanding person
    D. Assert his authority

6.____

7. Restating a question before the person being interviewed gives an answer to the original question is usually NOT good practice *principally* because
    A. the client will think that you don't know your job
    B. it may confuse the client
    C. the interviewer should know exactly what to ask and how to put the question
    D. it reveals the interviewer's insecurity

7.____

8. A white worker can BEST improve his ability to work with black clients if he
    A. tries to forget that the clients are black
    B. tells the black clients that he has no prejudices
    C. becomes aware of the problems black clients face
    D. socializes with black workers in the agency

8.____

9. A client warns that if he does not get what he wants he will report you to your supervisor and, if necessary, to the mayor's office. 9._____
Of the following, the MOST appropriate response for you to make in this situation is to

    A. encourage the client to do as he threatens because you know that you are right
    B. call your supervisor in so that the client may confront him
    C. explain to the client how the decision will be made on his request and suggest what action he can take if there is an adverse decision
    D. try to understand the client's problem but tell him that he must not explode in the office because you will have to ask him to leave if he does

Questions 10-20.

DIRECTIONS: Refer to the following Semi-Monthly Family Allowance Schedule and Conversion Table when answering Questions 10 through 20.

SEMI-MONTHLY FAMILY ALLOWANCE SCHEDULE
(Based on Number of Persons in Household)

NUMBER OF PERSONS IN HOUSEHOLD						
One	Two	Three	Four	Five	Six	Each Additional Person
$470.00	$750.00	$1000.00	$1290.00	$1590.00	$1840.00	$25.00

CONVERSION TABLE - WEEKLY TO SEMI-MONTHLY AMOUNTS

DOLLARS				CENTS			
Weekly Amount	Semi-Monthly Amount	Weekly Amount	Semi-Monthly Amount	Weekly Amount	Semi-Monthly Amount	Weekly Amount	Semi-Monthly Amount
$10.00	$21.70	$510.00	$1105.00	$0.10	$0.20	$5.10	$11.10
20.00	43.30	520.00	1126.70	0.20	0.40	5.20	11.30
30.00	65.00	530.00	1148.30	0.30	0.70	5.30	11.50
40.00	86.70	540.00	1170.00	0.40	0.90	5.40	11.70
50.00	108.30	550.00	1191.70	0.50	1.10	5.50	11.90
60.00	130.00	560.00	1213.30	0.60	1.30	5.60	12.10
70.00	151.70	570.00	1235.00	0.70	1.50	5.70	12.40
80.00	173.30	580.00	1256.70	0.80	1.70	5.80	12.60
90.00	195.00	590.00	1278.30	0.90	2.00	5.90	12.80
100.00	216.70	600.00	1300.00	1.00	2.20	6.00	13.00
110.00	238.30	610.00	1321.70	1.10	2.40	6.10	13.20
120.00	260.00	620.00	1343.30	1.20	2.60	6.20	13.40
130.00	281.70	630.00	1365.00	1.30	2.80	6.30	13.70
140.00	303.30	640.00	1386.70	1.40	3.00	6.40	13.90
150.00	325.00	650.00	1408.30	1.50	3.30	6.50	14.10
160.00	346.70	660.00	1430.00	1.60	3.50	6.60	14.30
170.00	368.30	670.00	1451.70	1.70	3.70	6.70	14.50
180.00	390.00	680.00	1473.30	1.80	3.90	6.80	14.70
190.00	411.70	690.00	1495.00	1.90	4.10	6.90	15.00
200.00	433.30	700.00	1516.70	2.00	4.30	7.00	15.20
210.00	455.00	710.00	1538.30	2.10	4.60	7.10	15.40
220.00	476.70	720.00	1560.00	2.20	4.80	7.20	15.60
230.00	498.30	730.00	1581.70	2.30	5.00	7.30	15.80
240.00	520.00	740.00	1603.30	2.40	5.20	7.40	16.00
250.00	541.70	750.00	1625.00	2.50	5.40	7.50	16.30
260.00	563.30	760.00	1646.70	2.60	5.60	7.60	16.50
270.00	585.00	770.00	1668.30	2.70	5.90	7.70	16.70
280.00	606.70	780.00	1690.00	2.80	6.10	7.80	16.90
290.00	628.30	790.00	1711.70	2.90	6.30	7.90	17.10
300.00	650.00	800.00	1733.30	3.00	6.50	8.00	17.30
310.00	671.70	810.00	1755.00	3.10	6.70	8.10	17.60
320.00	693.30	820.00	1776.70	3.20	6.90	8.20	17.80
330.00	715.00	830.00	1798.30	3.30	7.20	8.30	18.00
340.00	736.70	840.00	1820.00	3.40	7.40	8.40	18.20
350.00	783.00	850.00	1841.70	3.50	7.60	8.50	18.40
360.00	780.00	860.00	1863.30	3.60	7.80	8.60	18.60
370.00	801.70	870.00	1885.00	3.70	8.00	8.70	18.90
380.00	823.30	880.00	1906.70	3.80	8.20	8.80	19.10
390.00	845.00	890.00	1928.30	3.90	8.50	8.90	18.30
400.00	866.70	900.00	1950.00	4.00	8.70	9.00	19.50
410.00	888.30	910.00	1971.70	4.10	8.90	9.10	19.70
420.00	910.00	920.00	1993.30	4.20	9.10	9.20	19.90
430.00	931.70	930.00	2015.00	4.30	9.30	9.30	20.20
440.00	953.30	940.00	2036.70	4.40	9.50	9.40	20.40
450.00	975.00	950.00	2058.30	4.50	9.80	9.50	20.60
460.00	996.70	960.00	2080.00	4.60	10.00	9.60	20.80
470.00	1018.30	970.00	2101.70	4.70	10.20	9.70	21.00
480.00	1040.00	980.00	2123.30	4.80	10.40	9.80	21.20
490.00	1061.70	990.00	2145.00	4.90	10.60	9.90	21.50
500.00	1083.30	1000.00	2166.70	5.00	10.80		

NOTE: Questions 10 through 20 are to be answered SOLELY on the basis of the Schedule and Table given above and the information and case situations given below.

Questions 10 through 14 are based on Case Situation #1.
Questions 15 through 20 are based on Case Situation #2.

Public assistance grants are computed on a semi-monthly basis. This means that all figures are first broken down into semi-monthly amounts, and that when a client receives a check twice a month, each semi-monthly check covers his requirements for a period of approximately 2-1/6 weeks. The grants are computed by means of the following procedures.

1. Determine the semi-monthly allowance for the family from the Semi-Monthly Family Allowance Schedule.
2. Determine total semi-monthly income by deducting from the semi-monthly gross earnings (the wages or salary *before* payroll deductions) all semi-monthly expenses for federal, state, and city income taxes, Social Security payments, State Disability Insurance payments, union dues, cost of transportation, and $10.00 per work day for lunch.
3. Add the semi-monthly allowance and the semi-monthly rent (monthly rent must be divided in half).
4. Subtract the semi-monthly income (if there is any income).
5. The formula for computing the semi-monthly grant is:
   Family Allowance + Rent (semi-monthly)

   | Total Income | (semi-monthly) |
   | = Amount of Grant | (semi-monthly) |
6. Refer to the Conversion Table in order to convert weekly amounts into semi-monthly amounts.

CASE SITUATION #1

The Smiths receive public assistance. The family includes John Smith, his wife Barbara, and their four children. They occupy a five-room apartment for which the rent is $1050.00 per month. Mr. Smith is employed as a cleaner and his gross wages are $1000 per week. He is employed 5 days a week and spends $7.00 a day carfare. He buys his lunches. The following weekly deductions are made from his salary:

Social Security	$60.00
Disability Benefits	3.80
Federal Income Tax	43.00
State Income Tax	28.00
City Income Tax	10.00

CASE SITUATION #2

The Jones family receives public assistance. The family includes Steven and Diane Jones and their two children. They occupy a four-room apartment for which the rental is $850.00 a month. Mr. Jones is employed as a handyman, and his gross wages are $900 per week. He is employed 4 days a week and spends $7.00 a day carfare. He buys his lunches. He has the following weekly deductions made from his salary:

Social Security	$40.00
Disability Benefits	2.70
Federal Income Tax	38.90
State Income Tax	20.50
City Income Tax	6.20

10. The weekly amount that Mr. Smith contributes towards Social Security, Disability Benefits, and income taxes is   10.____
    A. $313.70   B. $231.40   C. $144.80   D. $106.80

11. The semi-monthly family allowance for the Smith family is   11.____
    A. $1290.00   B. $1590.00   C. $1840.00   D. $1845.00

12. What is the total of semi-monthly expenses related to Mr. Smith's employment which will be   12.____
    deducted from semi-monthly gross earnings to compute semi-monthly income?
    A. $497.80   B. $422.00   C. $389.50   D. $229.80

13. Which of the following amounts is the total semi-monthly income for the Smith family?   13.____
    A. $2166.70   B. $2000.00   C. $1668.90   D. $1004.40

14. The amount of the grant which the Smith family is entitled to receive is   14.____
    A. $2365.00   B. $1840.00   C. $1392.20   D. $696.10

15. The weekly amount that Mr. Jones contributes towards Social Security, Disability Benefits, and income taxes is   15.____
    A. $108.30   B. $176.30   C. $234.30   D. $234.70

16. The semi-monthly family allowance for the Jones family is   16.____
    A. $750.00   B. $1000.00   C. $1220.00   D. $1290.00

17. The total of semi-monthly expenses related to Mr. Jones' employment which will be   17.____
    deducted from semi-monthly gross earnings is
    A. $172.30   B. $189.30   C. $382.00   D. $407.20

18. Which of the following amounts is the total semi-monthly income for the Jones family?   18. ____
    A. $1282.00   B. $1553.20   C. $1568.00   D. $2122.30

19. The grant which the Jones family will receive is   19. ____
    A. $147.00   B. $294.00   C. $1290.00   D. $1715.00

20. If Mrs. Jones' monthly rent had been $1050, what would the amount of the grant be?   20. ____
    A. $247.00   B. $494.00   C. $772.00   D. $1822.00

———

KEY (CORRECT ANSWERS)

1.	A		11.	C
2.	B		12.	A
3.	D		13.	C
4.	A		14.	D
5.	A		15.	A
6.	B		16.	D
7.	B		17.	C
8.	C		18.	C
9.	C		19.	A
10.	C		20.	A

———

TEST 2

DIRECTIONS: Each question or incomplete statement is followed by several suggested answers or completions. Select the one that BEST answers the question or completes the statement. *PRINT THE LETTER OF THE CORRECT ANSWER IN THE SPACE AT THE RIGHT.*

Questions 1-5.

DIRECTIONS: Each of Questions 1 through 5 consists of information given in outline form and four sentences labeled A, B, C, and D. For each question, choose the one sentence which CORRECTLY expresses the information given in outline form and which also displays PROPER English usage.

1. Client's Name - Joanna Jones
   Number of Children - 3
   Client's Income - None
   Client's Marital Status - Single
   A.   Joanna Jones is an unmarried client with three children who have no income.
   B.   Joanna Jones, who is single and has no income, a client she has three children.
   C.   Joanna Jones, whose three children are clients, is single and has no income.
   D.   Joanna Jones, who has three children, is an unmarried client with no income.

1.____

2. Client's Name - Bertha Smith
   Number of Children - 2
   Client's Rent - $1050 per month
   Number of Rooms- 4
   A.   Bertha Smith, a client, pays $1050 per month for her four rooms with two children.
   B.   Client Bertha Smith has two children and pays $1050 per month for four rooms.
   C.   Client Bertha Smith is paying $1050 per month for two children with four rooms.
   D.   For four rooms and two children, Client Bertha Smith pays $1050 per month.

2.____

3. Name of Employee - Cynthia Dawes
   Number of Cases Assigned - 9
   Date Cases Were Assigned - 12/16
   Number of Assigned Cases Completed - 8
   A.   On December 16, employee Cynthia Dawes was assigned nine cases; she has completed eight of these cases.
   B.   Cynthia Dawes, employee on December 16, assigned nine cases, completed eight.
   C.   Being employed on December 16, Cynthia Dawes completed eight of nine assigned cases.
   D.   Employee Cynthia Dawes, she was assigned nine cases and completed eight, on December 16.

3.____

4. Place of Audit - Broadway Center
   Names of Auditors - Paul Cahn, Raymond Perez
   Date of Audit - 11/20
   Number of Cases Audited - 41
   A.   On November 20, at the Broadway Center 41 cases was audited by auditors Paul Cahn and Raymond Perez.
   B.   Auditors Raymond Perez and Paul Cahn has audited 41 cases at the Broadway

4.____

Center, on November 20.

   C. At the Broadway Center, on November 20, auditors Paul Cahn and Raymond Perez audited 41 cases.

   D. Auditors Paul Cahn and Raymond Perez at the Broadway Center, on November 20, is auditing 41 cases.

5. Name of Client - Barbra Levine   5.____

    Client's Monthly Income - $2100

    Client's Monthly Expenses - $4520

   A. Barbra Levine is a client, her monthly income is $2100 and her monthly expenses is $4520.

   B. Barbra Levine's monthly income is $2100 and she is a client, with whose monthly expenses are $4520.

   C. Barbra Levine is a client whose monthly income is $2100 and whose monthly expenses are $4520.

   D. Barbra Levine, a client, is with a monthly income which is $2100 and monthly expenses which are $4520.

Questions 6-10.

DIRECTIONS: Questions 6 through 10 are to be answered SOLELY on the basis of the information contained in the following passage.

Any person who is living in New York City and is otherwise eligible may be granted public assistance whether or not he has New York State residence. However, since New York City does not contribute to the cost of assistance granted to persons who are without State residence, the cases of all recipients must be formally identified as to whether or not each member of the household has State residence.

To acquire State residence a person must have resided in New York State continuously for one year. Such residence is not lost unless the person is out of the State continuously for a period of one year or longer. Continuous residence does not include any period during which the individual is a patient in a hospital, an inmate of a public institution or of an incorporated private institution, a resident on a military reservation or a minor residing in a boarding home while under the care of an authorized agency. Receipt of public assistance does not prevent a person from acquiring State residence. State residence, once acquired, is not lost because of absence from the State while a person is serving in the U.S. Armed Forces or the Merchant Marine; nor does a member of the family of such a person lose State residence while living with or near that person in these circumstances.

Each person, regardless of age, acquires or loses State residence as an individual. There is no derivative State residence except for an infant at the time of birth. He is deemed to have State residence if he is in the custody of both parents and either one of them has State residence, or if the parent having custody of him has State residence.

6. According to the above passage, an infant is deemed to have New York State residence at the time of his birth *if*

    A. he is born in New York State but neither of his parents is a resident

    B. he is in the custody of only one parent, who is not a resident, but his other parent is a resident

    C. his brother and sister are residents

    D. he is in the custody of both his parents but only one of them is a resident

6.____

7. The Jones family consists of five members. Jack and Mary Jones have lived in New York State continuously for the past eighteen months after having lived in Ohio since they were born. Of their three children, one was born ten months ago and has been in the custody of his parents since birth. Their second child lived in Ohio until six months ago and then moved in with his parents. Their third child had never lived in New York until he moved with his parents to New York eighteen months ago. However, he entered the armed forces one month later and has not lived in New York since that time.

Based on the above passage, how many members of the Jones family are New York State residents?

    A. 2   B. 3   C. 4   D. 5

7.____

8. Assuming that each of the following individuals has lived continuously in New York State for the past year, and has never previously lived in the State, which one of them is a New York State resident?

    A. Jack Salinas, who has been an inmate in a State correctional facility for six months of the year

    B. Fran Johnson, who has lived on an Army base for the entire year

    C. Arlene Snyder, who married a non-resident during the past year

    D. Gary Phillips, who was a patient in a Veterans Administration hospital for the entire year

8.____

9. The above passage implies that the reason for determining whether or not a recipient of public assistance is a State resident is that

    A. the cost of assistance for non-residents is not a New York City responsibility

    B. non-residents living in New York City are not eligible for public assistance

    C. recipients of public assistance are barred from acquiring State residence

    D. New York City is responsible for the full cost of assistance to recipients who are residents

9.____

10. Assume that the Rollins household in New York City consists of six members at the present time - Anne Rollins, her three children, her aunt and her uncle. Anne Rollins and one of her children moved to New York City seven months ago. Neither of them had previously lived in New York State. Her other two children have lived in New York City continuously for the past two years, as has her aunt. Anne Rollins' uncle had lived in New York City continuously for many years until two years ago. He then entered the armed forces and has returned to New York City within the past month.

Based on the above passage, how many members of the Rollins' household are New York State residents?

    A. 2   B. 3   C. 4   D. 6

10.____

11. You are interviewing a client to determine whether financial assistance should be continued and you find that what he is telling you does not agree exactly with your records.
Of the following, the BEST way to handle this situation is to
    A. recommend that his public assistance payments be stopped, since you have caught him lying to you
    B. tell the client about the points of disagreement and ask him if he can clear them up
    C. give the client the benefit of the doubt and recommend continuation of his payments
    D. show the client the records and warn him that he must either tell the truth or lose his benefits

11.____

12. An applicant for public assistance gets angry at some of the questions you must ask her.
Of the following, the BEST way to handle this situation is to
    A. assume that she is trying to hide something, and end the interview
    B. skip the questions that bother her and come back to them at the end of the interview
    C. tell her that she must either answer the question or leave
    D. explain to her that you are required to get answers to all the questions in order to be able to help her

12.____

13. At the end of an interview to determine whether financial assistance should be continued, the client offers to take you to lunch.
Of the following, the BEST response to such an invitation is to
    A. tell the client that you do not take bribes and report the matter to your supervisor
    B. accept the invitation if you have the time, but do not let it influence your recommendation as to his eligibility for continuing public assistance
    C. politely refuse the invitation, and do not let it influence your recommendation as to his continuing eligibility for public assistance
    D. point out to the client that his budget does not include money for entertainment

13.____

Questions 14-18.

DIRECTIONS: Questions 14 through 18 are to be answered SOLELY on the basis of the information, the assumptions, and the table given below.

    Each question describes an applicant family. You are to determine into which of the four categories (A, B, C, or D) each of the applicant families should be placed. In order to do this, you must match the description of the applicant family with the factors determining eligibility for each of the four categories. Each applicant family must meet ALL of the criteria for the category.

ASSUMPTIONS FOR ALL QUESTIONS
    The information in the following tables does NOT necessarily reflect actual practice in the Department of Social Services.
    1.   The date of application is January 25.
        Each applicant family that cannot be placed in categories A, B, or C must be placed in category D.
    2.   A *dependent child* is a child who is less than 18 years of age, or less than 21 years of age if attending school full time, who depends upon its parents for support.
    3.   A mother in a family with one or more dependent children is not expected to work and her work status is not to be considered in establishing the category of the family.

CATEGORY OF APPLICANT FAMILY	FACTORS DETERMINING ELIGIBILITY

A	1. There is at least one dependent child in the home.
	2. Children are deprived of parental support because father is:
	   (a) Deceased
	   (b) Absent from the home
	   (c) Incapacitated due to medically verified illness
	   (d) Over age 65
	   (e) Not fully employed because of verified ill health
	3. Parents or guardians reside in the same home as the children.
	4. Applicant family must have resided in the State for a period of one year or more.

B	1. There is at least one dependent child in the home. 2. Both parents are in the home and are not incapacitated. 3. Both parents are the children's natural parents. 4. Father unemployed or works less than 70 hours per month. 5. Father has recent work history. 6. Father not currently receiving Unemployment Insurance Benefits. 7. Father available and willing to work. 8. Applicant family must have resided in the State for a period of one year or more.
C	1. There is a war veteran in the home. 2. Applicant families do not meet the criteria for Categories A or B.
D	Applicant families do not meet the criteria for Categories A, B, or C

14. Woman, aged 52, with child 6 years old who she states was left in her home at the age of 2. Woman states child is her niece, and that she has no knowledge of whereabouts of parents or any other relatives. Both woman and child have resided in the State since June 15.   14. ____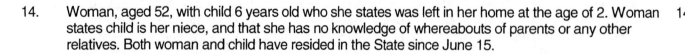

15. Married couple with 2 dependent children at home. Family has resided in the State for the last 5 years. Wife cannot work. Husband, veteran of Gulf War, can work only 15 hours a week due to kidney ailment (verified).   15. ____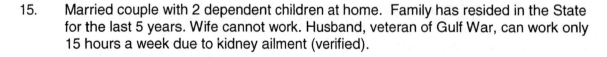

16. Married couple, both aged 35, with 3 dependent children at home, 1 of whom is 17 years of age. Wife available for work and presently working 2 days a week, 7 hours each day. Husband, who was laid off two weeks ago, is not eligible for Unemployment Insurance Benefits. Family has resided in the State since January 1, 2002.

16.____

17. Married couple with 1 dependent child at home. They have resided in the State since January 25, 2001. Wife must remain home to take care of child. Husband veteran of Gulf War. Husband is available for work on a limited basis because of heart condition which has been verified. A second child, a married 17-year-old son, lives in California.

17.____

18. Married couple with 2 children, ages 6 and 12, at home. Family has resided in the State since June 2, 1998. Wife not available for work. Husband, who served in the Iraqi War, was laid off 3 weeks ago and is receiving Unemployment Insurance Benefits of $500.00 weekly.

18.____

19. Of the following, the MOST important reason for referring a public assistance client for employment or training is to
    A. give him self-confidence
    B. make him self-supporting
    C. have him learn a new trade
    D. take him off the streets

19.____

20. Sometimes clients become silent during interviews.
    Of the following, the MOST probable reason for such silence is that the client is
    A. getting ready to tell a lie
    B. of low intelligence and does not know the answers to your questions
    C. thinking things over or has nothing more to say on the subject
    D. wishing he were not on welfare

20.____

KEY (CORRECT ANSWERS)

1.	D	6.	D	11.	B	16.	B
2.	B	7.	B	12.	D	17.	A
3.	A	8.	C	13.	C	18.	C
4.	C	9.	A	14.	D	19.	B
5.	C	10.	C	15.	A	20.	C

EXAMINATION SECTION
TEST 1

DIRECTIONS: Each question or incomplete statement is followed by several suggested answers or completions. Select the l one that BEST answers the question or completes the statement. *PRINT THE LETTER OF THE CORRECT ANSWER IN THE SPACE AT THE RIGHT.*

1.   The applicant you are interviewing is a man in his late forties who has recently lost his job and has a family of eight to support. He is very upset and tells you he does not know where he will get the money to purchase food for the family and pay the rent. He does not know what he will do if he is found not eligible for public assistance. He asks you whether you think he will be eligible. You feel the applicant has a good chance, and you think he should receive financial assistance, but you are not completely certain that he is eligible for public assistance under departmental policy.
Of the following, the BEST action for you to take is to   1._____

   A.   reassure the applicant and tell him you are sure everything will be all right because there is no sense in worrying him before you know for certain that he is not eligible
   B.   tell the applicant that as far as you are concerned he should receive public assistance but that you are not certain the department will go along with your recommendation
   C.   tell the applicant that you are not sure that he will be found eligible for public assistance
   D.   adopt a cool manner and tell the applicant that he must behave like an adult and not allow himself to become emotional about the situation

2.   When conducting an interview with a client receiving public assistance, it would be LEAST important for you to try to   2._____

   A.   understand the reasons for the client's statements
   B.   conduct the interview on the client's intellectual level
   C.   imitate the client's speech as much as possible
   D.   impress the client with the agency's concern for his welfare

Questions 3-6.

DIRECTIONS: Questions 3 through 6 are to be answered SOLELY on basis of the following case history of the Foster family.

FOSTER CASE HISTORY

Form W-341-C	Date: Jan. 25, 2005
Rev. 3/1/93	Case Name: Foster
600M-804077-S-200 (93)-245	Case No. : ADC-3415968

Family Composition:
Ann Foster,	b. 7.23.67
Gerry	b. 1.7.92
Susan	b. 4.1.94
John	b. 5.3.97
Joan	b. 10.14.00

Mrs. Foster was widowed in June 2001 when her husband was killed in a car accident. Since that time, the family has received public assistance. Mrs. Foster has been referred for housekeeping service by the Social Service Department of Lincoln Hospital, where she is being treated in the neurology clinic. Her primary diagnosis is multiple sclerosis. The hospital reports that she is going through a period of deterioration characterized by an unsteady gait, and weakness and tremor in the limbs. At this time, her capacity to manage a household and four children is severely limited. She feels quite overwhelmed and is unable to function adequately in taking care of her home.

In addition to the medical reasons, it is advisable that a housekeeper be placed in the home as part of a total plan to avoid further family breakdown and deterioration. This deterioration is reflected by all family members. Mrs. Foster is severely depressed and is unable to meet the needs of her children, who have a variety of problems. Joan, the youngest, is not speaking, is hyperactive, and in general is not developing normally for a child her age. John is showing learning problems in school and has poor articulation. Susan was not promoted last year and is a behavior problem at home. Gerry, the oldest, is deformed due to a fire at age two. It is clear that Mrs. Foster cannot control or properly discipline her children, but even more important is the fact that she is unable to offer them the encouragement and guidance they require.

It is hoped that providing housekeeping service will relieve Mrs. Foster of the basic household chores so that she will be less frustrated and better able to provide the love and guidance needed by her children.

3. The age of the child who is described as not developing normally, hyperactive, and not speaking is   3.____

    A. 4   B. 7   C. 10   D. 13

4. Which of the following CANNOT be verified on the basis of the Foster Case History above?   4.____

    A. William Foster was Ann Foster's husband.
    B. Mrs. Foster has been seen in the neurology clinic at Lincoln Hospital.
    C. John Foster has trouble with his speech.
    D. The Foster family has received public assistance since June 2001.

5. The form on which the information about the Foster family is presented is known as   5.____

    A. Family Composition Form   B. Form Rev. 3/1/93
    C. Form W-341-C   D. ADC-3415968

6. According to the above case history, housekeeping service is being requested PRIMA-   6.____
   RILY because

   A. no one in the family can perform the household chores
   B. Mrs. Foster suffers from multiple sclerosis and requires assistance with the house-
      hold chores
   C. the children are exhibiting behavior problems resulti from the mother's illness
   D. the children have no father

7. You notice that an applicant whom you rejected for public assistance is back at the center   7.____
   the following morning and is waiting to be interviewed by another worker in your group.
   Of the following, the BEST approach for you to take is to

   A. inform the worker, before she interviews the applican that you had interviewed and
      rejected him the previou day
   B. not inform the worker about the situation and let her make her own decision
   C. approach the applicant and tell him he was rejected for good reason and will have
      to leave the center immediately
   D. ask the special officer at the center to remove the applicant

8. You have just finished interviewing an applicant who has a violent temper and has dis-   8.____
   played a great amount of hostility toward you during the interview. You find he is ineligible
   for public assistance. Departmental policy is that all applicants are notified by mail in a
   day or so of their acceptance or rejection for public assistance. However, you also have
   the option, if you think it is desirable, of notifying the applicant at the interview.
   Of the following, the BEST action for you to take in this case is to

   A. tell the applicant of his rejection during the interview
   B. have the applicant notified of the results of the interview by mail only
   C. ask your supervisor to inform the applicant of his rejection
   D. inform the applicant of the results of the interview, with a special patrolman at your
      side

9. You are interviewing a client who speaks English poorly and whose native language is   9.____
   Spanish. Your knowledge of Spanish is very limited.
   Of the following, the FIRST action it would be best for you to take is to

   A. try to locate a worker at the center who speaks Spani
   B. write our your questions because it is easier for people to understand a new lan-
      guage when it is written rather than when it is spoken
   C. do the best you can, using hand gestures to make yourself understood
   D. tell the client to return with a friend or relative who speaks English

10. During an interview with a client of another race, he accuses you of racial prejudice and   10.____
    asks for an interviewer of his own race.
    Of the following, which is the BEST way to handle the situation?

    A. In a friendly manner, tell the client that eligibility is based on the regulations and the
       facts, not on prejudice, and ask him to continue with the interview.
    B. Explain to your supervisor that you cannot deal with someone who accuses you of
       prejudice, and ask your supervisor to assign the client someone of his own race.
    C. Assure the client that you will lean over backwards to treat his application favorably.

D. Tell the client that some of your friends are of his race and that you could therefore not possibly be prejudiced.

Questions 11-15.

DIRECTIONS: In order to answer Questions 11 through 15, assume that you have been asked to write a short report on the basis of the information contained in the following passage about the granting of emergency funds to the Smith family.

Mr. and Mrs. Smith, who have been receiving public assistance for the last six months, arrive at the center the morning of August 2, totally upset and anxious because they and their family have been burned out of their apartment the night before. The fire seems to have been of suspicious origin because at the time it broke out witnesses spotted two neighborhood teenagers running away from the scene. The policemen, who arrived at the scene shortly after the firemen, took down the pertinent information about the alleged arsonists.

The Smiths have spent the night with friends but now request emergency housing and emergency funds for themselves and their four children to purchase food and to replace the clothing which was destroyed by the fire. The burned-out apartment had consisted of 5 rooms and a bath, and the Smiths are now worried that they will be forced to accept smaller accommodations. Furthermore, since Mrs. Smith suffers from a heart murmur, she is worried that their new living quarters will necessitate her climbing too many stairs. Her previous apartment was a one-flight walk-up, which was acceptable.

As the worker in charge, you have studied the case, determined the amount of the emergency grant, made temporary arrangements for the Smiths to stay at a hotel, and reassured Mrs. Smith that everything possible will be done to find them an apartment which will meet with their approval.

11. Which of the following would it be BEST to include in the report as the reason for the emergency grant?

    A. The police have decided that the fire is of suspicious origin.
    B. Two neighborhood teenagers were seen leaving the fire at the Smiths'.
    C. The apartment of the Smith family has been destroyed by fire.
    D. Mrs. Smith suffers from a heart murmur and cannot climb stairs.

11.____

12. Which of the following would it be BEST to accept as verification of the fire?
A

    A. letter from the friends with whom the Smiths stayed the previous night
    B. photograph of the fire
    C. dated newspaper clipping describing the fire
    D. note from the Smiths' neighbors

12.____

13. A report of the Smith family's need for a new apartment must be sent to the center's housing specialist.
    Which of the following recommendations for housing would be MOST appropriate?

    A. Two bedrooms, first floor walk-up
    B. Five rooms, ground floor
    C. Two-room suite, hotel with elevator
    D. Three rooms, building with elevator

13.____

14. For which of the following are the Smiths requesting emergency funds? 14.____

    A. Furniture   B. Food
    C. A hotel room   D. Repairs in their apartment

15. Which of the following statements provides the BEST summary of the action taken by 15.____
you on the Smith case and is MOST important for inclusion in your report?

    A. Mr. and Mrs. Smith arrived upset and anxious and were reassured.
    B. It was verified that there was a fire.
    C. Temporary living arrangements were made, and the amount of the emergency
        grant was determined.
    D. The case was studied and a new apartment was found for the Smiths which met
        with their approval.

16. It is important that you remember what has happened between you and a client during 16.____
an interview so that you may deliver appropriate services.
However, the one of the following which is the MOST likely reason that taking notes
during the interview may not always be a good practice is that

    A. you may lose the notes and have to go back and see the client again
    B. some clients may believe that you are not interested in what they are saying
    C. you are the only one who is likely to read the notes
    D. some clients may believe that you are not smart enough to remember what hap-
        pened in the interview

17. Before an applicant seeking public assistance can be interviewed, he must fill out a com- 17.____
plex application form which consists of eleven pages of questions requesting very
detailed information.
Of the following, the BEST time for you to review the information on the application
form is

    A. before she begins to interview the applicant
    B. after she has asked the applicant a few questions to put him at ease
    C. towards the end of the interview so that she has a chance to think about the infor-
        mation received during the interview
    D. after the interview has been completed

Questions 18-20.

DIRECTIONS: In Questions 18 through 20, choose the lettered word which means MOST
                 NEARLY the same as the underlined word in the sentence.

18. He needed public assistance because he was incapacitated. The word incapacitated 18.____
means MOST NEARLY

    A. uneducated   B. disabled
    C. uncooperative   D. discharged

19. The caseworker explained to the client that signing the document was compulsory. 19.____
The word compulsory means MOST NEARLY

    A. temporary   B. required
    C. different   D. comprehensive

20. The woman's actions did not <u>jeopardize</u> her eligibility for benefits.
     The word <u>jeopardize</u> means MOST NEARLY

    A. delay   B. reinforce   C. determine   D. endanger

20.____

KEY (CORRECT ANSWERS)

1.	C	11.	C
2.	C	12.	C
3.	A	13.	B
4.	A	14.	B
5.	C	15.	C
6.	B	16.	B
7.	A	17.	A
8.	B	18.	B
9.	A	19.	B
10.	A	20.	D

TEST 2

DIRECTIONS: Each question or incomplete statement is followed by several suggested answers or completions. Select the one that BEST answers the question or completes the statement. *PRINT THE LETTER OF THE CORRECT ANSWER IN THE SPACE AT THE RIGHT.*

Questions 1-4.

DIRECTIONS: Questions 1 through 4 are to be answered on the basis of the information given in the Fact Situation and Sample Form below.

FACT SITUATION

On October 7, 2004, John Smith (Case #ADC-U 1467912) applied and was accepted for public assistance for himself and his family. His family consists of his wife, Helen, and their children: William, age 9; John Jr., age 6; and Mary, age 2. The family has lived in a five-room apartment located at 142 West 137 Street, Manhattan, since July 18, 1998. Mr. Smith signed a 2-year lease for this apartment on July 18, 2004 at a rent of $500 per month. The maximum rental allowance for a family of this size is $420 per month. Utilities are included in this rent-controlled multiple dwelling.

Since the cost of renting this apartment is in excess of the allowable amount, the Supervising Clerk (Income Maintenance) is required to fill out a "Request for Approval of Exception to Policy for Shelter Allowance/Rehousing Expenses."

A sample of a section of this form follows.

SAMPLE FORM

REQUEST FOR APPROVAL OF EXCEPTION TO POLICY FOR SHELTER ALLOWANCE /REHOUSING EXPENSES

Case Name	Case No. or Pending		Acceptance Date		Group No.	
Present Address ZIP	Apt. No. or Location	No. of Rooms	Rent per Mo. $		Occupancy Date	
HOUSEHOLD COMPOSITION (List all persons living in the household) Column I Surname First	Col. 2 Birth-date	Col. 3 Sex	Column 4 Relation to Case Head	Column 5 Marital Status	Column 6 P. A. Status	

1. Based on the information given in the Fact Situation, which one of the following should be entered in the space for *Occupancy Date?*　　1.____

    A. October 7, 2004　　　　　　　　B. July 18, 2004
    C. July 18, 1998　　　　　　　　　　D. Unknown

2. What amount should be entered in the space labeled *Rent per Mo. ?*　　2.____

    A. $500　　　　　B. $420　　　　　C. $300　　　　　D. $80

3. Based on the information given in the Fact Situation, it is IMPOSSIBLE to fill in which one of the following blanks?　　3.____

    A. *Case Number or pending*　　　　B. *Acceptance Date*
    C. *Apt. No. or Location*　　　　　　D. *No. of Rooms*

4. Which of the following should be entered in Column 4 for Helen Smith?　　4.____

    A. Wife　　　　　B. Head　　　　　C. Mother　　　　　D. Unknown

Questions 5-13.

DIRECTIONS:　In Questions 5 through 13, perform the computations indicated and choose the CORRECT answer from the four choices given.

5. Add $4.34, $34.50, $6.00, $101.76, $90.67. From the result, subtract $60.54 and $10.56.　　5.____

    A. $76.17　　　　B. $156.37　　　　C. $166.17　　　　D. $300.37

6. Add 2,200, 2,600, 252, and 47.96.　　6.____
  From the result, subtract 202.70, 1,200, 2,150, and 434.43.

    A. 1,112.83　　　B. 1,213.46　　　C. 1,341.51　　　D. 1,348.91

7. Multiply 1850 by .05 and multiply 3300 by .08 and then add both results.　　7.____

    A. 242.50　　　　B. 264.00　　　　C. 333.25　　　　D. 356.50

8. Multiply 312.77 by .04.　　8.____
  Round off the result to the nearest hundredth.

    A. 12.52　　　　B. 12.511　　　　C. 12.518　　　　D. 12.51

9. Add 362.05, 91.13, 347.81, and 17.46, and then divide the result by 6.　　9.____
  The answer rounded off to the nearest hundredth is

    A. 138.409　　　B. 137.409　　　C. 136.41　　　D. 136.40

10. Add 66.25 and 15.06, and then multiply the result by 2 1/6.　　10.____
  The answer is MOST NEARLY

    A. 176.18　　　　B. 176.17　　　　C. 162.66　　　　D. 162.62

11. Each of the following options contains three decimals. In which case do all three decimals have the same value?　　11.____

    A. .3; .30; .03　　　　　　　　　　B. .25; .250; .2500
    C. 1.9; 1.90; 1.09　　　　　　　　D. .35; .350; .035

12. Add 1/2 the sum of (539.84 and 479.26) to 1/3 the sum of (1461.93 and 927.27).   12._____
Round off the result to the nearest whole number.

    A. 3408   B. 2899   C. 1816   D. 1306

13. Multiply $5,906.09 by 15%, and then divide the result by 1/3.   13._____

    A. $295.30   B. $885.91   C. $8,859.14   D. $29,530.45

Questions 14-18.

DIRECTIONS: Questions 14 through 18 are to be answered SOLELY on the basis of the information provided in the following passage.

The ideal relationship for the interview is one of mutual confidence. To try to pretend, to put on a front of cordiality and friendship is extremely unwise for the interviewer because he will certainly convey, by subtle means, his real feelings. It is the interviewer's responsibility to take the lead in establishing a relationship of mutual confidence.

As the interviewer, you should help the interviewee to feel at ease and ready to talk. One of the best ways to do this is to be at ease yourself. If you are, it will probably be evident; if you are not, it will almost certainly be apparent to the interviewee.

Begin the interview with topics for discussion which are easy to talk about and non-menacing. This interchange can be like the conversation of people when they are waiting for a bus, at the ball game, or discussing the weather. However, do not prolong this warm-up too long since the interviewee knows as well as you do that these are not the things he came to discuss. Delaying too long in getting down to business may suggest to him that you are reluctant to deal with the topic.

Once you get onto the main topics, do all that you can to get the interviewee to talk freely with as little prodding from you as possible. This will probably require that you give him some idea of the area, and of ways of looking at it. Avoid, however, prejudicing or coloring his remarks by what you say; especially, do not in any way indicate that there are certain things you want to hear, others which you do not want to hear. It is essential that he feel free to express his own ideas unhampered by your ideas, your values and preconceptions.

Do not appear to dominate the interview, nor have even the suggestion of a patronizing attitude. Ask some questions which will enable the interviewee to take pride in his knowledge. Take the attitude that the interviewee sincerely wants the interview to achieve its purpose. This creates a warm, permissive atmosphere that is most important in all interviews.

14. Of the following, the BEST title for the above passage is   14._____

    A.   PERMISSIVENESS IN INTERVIEWING
    B.   INTERVIEWING TECHNIQUES
    C.   THE FACTOR OF PRETENSE IN THE INTERVIEW
    D.   THE CORDIAL INTERVIEW

15. Which of the following recommendations on the conduct of an interview is made by the above passage?　　　15.____

    A. Conduct the interview as if it were an interchange between people discussing the weather.
    B. The interview should be conducted in a highly impersonal manner.
    C. Allow enough time for the interview so that the interviewee does not feel rushed.
    D. Start the interview with topics which are not threatening to the interviewee.

16. The above passage indicates that the interviewer should　　　16.____

    A. feel free to express his opinions
    B. patronize the interviewee and display a permissive attitude
    C. permit the interviewee to give the needed information in his own fashion
    D. provide for privacy when conducting the interview

17. The meaning of the word *unhampered,* as it is used in the last sentence of the fourth paragraph of the preceding passage, is MOST NEARLY　　　17.____

    A. unheeded　　　　　　　　B. unobstructed
    C. hindered　　　　　　　　　D. aided

18. It can be INFERRED from the above passage that　　　18.____

    A. interviewers, while generally mature, lack confidence
    B. certain methods in interviewing are more successful than others in obtaining information
    C. there is usually a reluctance on the part of interviewers to deal with unpleasant topics
    D. it is best for the interviewer not to waiver from the use of hard and fast rules when dealing with clients

19. The applicant whom you are interviewing is not talking rationally, and he admits that he is under the influence of alcohol.
Which of the following is the BEST way of handling this situation?　　　19.____

    A. Call a security guard and have the applicant removed.
    B. Tell the applicant that unless he gets control of himself, he will not receive financial assistance.
    C. Send out for a cup of black coffee for the applicant.
    D. End the interview and plan to schedule another appointment.

20. During an interview, an applicant who has submitted an application for assistance breaks down and cries. Of the following, the BEST way of handling this situation is to　　　20.____

    A. end the interview and schedule a new appointment
    B. be patient and sympathetic, and encourage the applicant to continue the interview
    C. tell the applicant sternly that crying will not help matters
    D. tell the applicant that you will do everything you can to get the application approved

KEY (CORRECT ANSWERS)

1.	C	11.	B
2.	A	12.	D
3.	C	13.	A
4.	A	14.	B
5.	C	15.	D
6.	A	16.	C
7.	D	17.	B
8.	D	18.	B
9.	C	19.	D
10.	B	20.	B

EXAMINATION SECTION
TEST 1

DIRECTIONS: Each question or incomplete statement is followed by several suggested answers or completions. Select the one that *BEST* answers the question or completes the statement. *PRINT THE LETTER OF THE CORRECT ANSWER IN THE SPACE AT THE RIGHT.*

1. A client tells you that he is extremely upset by the treatment that he received from Center personnel at the information desk.
Which of the following is the *BEST* way to handle this complaint during the interview?

    A.   Explain to the client that he probably misinterpreted what occurred at the information desk
    B.   Let the client express his feelings and then proceed with the interview
    C.   Tell the client that you are not concerned with the personnel at the information desk
    D.   Escort the client to the information desk to find out what really happened

1.____

2. As a worker in the foster home division, you are reviewing a case record to determine whether a 13-year-old boy, in foster care because of neglect and mistreatment by his natural parents, should be returned home. The natural parents, who want to take the child back, have been in family counseling, with encouraging results, and have improved their living conditions.
Of the following, it would be appropriate to recommend that the child

    A.   remain with the foster parents, since this is a documented case of child abuse
    B.   remain with the foster parents until they are ready to send him home
    C.   be returned to his natural parents, since they have made positive efforts to change their behavior toward the child
    D.   be returned to his natural parents, because continued separation will cause irreparable damage to the child

2.____

3. You are finishing an interview with a client in which you have explained to her the procedure she must go through to apply for income maintenance.
Of the following, the *BEST* way for you to make sure that she has fully understood the procedure is to ask her

    A.   whether she feels she has understood your explanation of the procedure
    B.   whether she has any questions to ask you about the procedure
    C.   to describe the procedure to you in her own words
    D.   a few questions to test her understanding of the procedure

3.____

4. Mrs. Carey, a widow with five children, has come to the field office to seek foster care for her 13-year-old daughter, who has often been truant from school and has recently been caught shoplifting. Mrs. Carey says that she cannot maintain a proper home environment for the other four children and deal with her daughter at the same time.
Of the following, you should *FIRST*

    A.   process Mrs. Carey's request for placement of her daughter in a foster care agency
    B.   interview both Mrs. Carey and her daughter to get a more complete picture of the situation
    C.   suggest to Mrs. Carey that she might be able to manage if she obtained homemaker services
    D.   warn the daughter that she will be sent away from home if she does not change her behavior

4.____

5. During a group orientation meeting with couples who wish to adopt babies through your agency, one couple asks you how they should deal with the question of whether the child should be told that he is adopted.
   Of the following, your BEST response to this couple is to

   A. tell them to conceal from the child the fact that he is adopted
   B. suggest that they lead the child to believe that his natural parents are dead
   C. tell them to inform the child that they know nothing about his natural parents
   D. explore with them their feelings about revealing to the child that he is adopted

6. You are beginning an investigation of an anonymous complaint that a welfare client has a concealed bank account. Of the following, the FIRST step you should generally take in conducting this investigation is to

   A. confront the client with the complaint during an office interview
   B. try to track down the source of the anonymous complaint
   C. make a surprise visit to the client in his home to question him
   D. gather any available information from bank and agency records

7. When investigating the location of an absent parent, the worker frequently interviews the parent's friends and neighbors. The worker often writes down the information given by the person interviewed and, at the end of the interview, summarizes the information to the person.
   For the worker to do this is, generally,

   A. *good practice,* because the person interviewed will be Impressed by the efficiency of the worker
   B. *poor practice,* because the person interviewed may become impatient with the worker for repeating the information
   C. *good practice,* because the person interviewed has an opportunity to correct any errors the worker may have in recording the information
   D. *poor practice,* because summarizing the information may encourage the person to waste time adding and changing information

8. During an interview for the purpose of investigating a charge of child abuse, a client first denied that she had abused her child, but then burst into tears and promised that she *will never do it again.*
   Of the following, the MOST appropriate action for the worker to take in this situation is to

   A. tell the client that, since she has already lied, it is difficult to believe that she will keep her promise
   B. show a concern for the client's feelings but tell her that you will have to report your findings and refer her for help
   C. determine the extent to which the child was abused and close the case if no permanent harm was done
   D. explain to the client that she has already done enough harm to the child and you must, therefore, recommend placement

9. As a worker involved in locating absent parents, you have obtained information indicating that the address for the putative father is the same as the client's address. In order to determine whether, in fact, the client and putative father are living together, of the following, it would be MOST appropriate to

    A. visit the address and question the neighbors and superintendent about the putative father

    B. visit the client to ask her why she has concealed the fact that the putative father is living with her

    C. file the information in the case folder and wait for confirming information

    D. close the client's case and issue a recoupment notice to the putative father

10. A client claims that she never received a welfare check that was due her. As part of your investigation of her claim, you obtain from the bank a copy of the check, which has been endorsed with her name and cashed.
Of the following, the *BEST* procedure for you to follow in this investigation is to

    A. end the investigation immediately, since the client's claim cannot be proved

    B. interview the client and show her the copy of the cashed check

    C. tell the client that you have evidence that her claim is false

    D. say nothing about the cashed check and try to trap the client in a false statement

10.____

11. As part of the investigation to locate an absent father, you make a field visit to interview one of the father's friends. Before beginning the interview, you identify yourself to the friend and show him your official identification.
For you to do this is, generally,

    A. *good practice,* because the friend will have proof that you are authorized to make such confidential investigations

    B. *poor practice,* because the friend may not answer your questions when he knows why you are interviewing him

    C. *good practice,* because your supervisor can confirm from the friend that you actually made the interview

    D. *poor practice,* because the friend may warn the absent father that your agency is looking for him

11.____

12. As a field office worker you are investigating a citizen's complaint charging a mother of three children with child neglect. The mother tells you that her husband has become depressed after losing his job and is often abusive to her, and that this situation has made her feel anxious and has made it difficult for her to care for the children properly.
Which one of the following is the *BEST* way for you to respond to this situation?

    A. Tell the mother that she must do everything possible to help her husband find a job

    B. Arrange to meet the husband so you can explain to him the consequences of his behavior

    C. Investigate the complaint, report your findings, and refer the family for counseling or other appropriate services

    D. Suggest that the family obtain homemaker services so that the mother can go to work

12.____

13. You are interviewing a client in his home as part of your investigation of an anonymous complaint that he has been receiving Medicaid fraudulently. During the interview, the client frequently interrupts your questions to discuss the hardships of his life and the bitterness he feels about his medical condition.
Of the following, the *BEST* way for you to deal with these discussions is to

    A. cut them off abruptly, since the client is probably just trying to avoid answering your questions

13.____

B. listen patiently, since these discussions may be helpful to the client and may give you information for your investigation

C. remind the client that you are investigating a complaint against him and he must answer directly

D. seek to gain the client's confidence by discussing any personal or medical problems which you yourself may have

14. While interviewing an absent father to determine his ability to pay child support, you realize that his answers to some of your questions contradict his answers to other questions. Of the following, the *BEST* way for you to try to get accurate information from the father is to

    14._____

    A. confront him with his contradictory answers and demand an explanation from him

    B. use your best judgment as to which of his answers are accurate and question him accordingly

    C. tell him that he has misunderstood your questions and that he must clarify his answers

    D. ask him the same questions in different words and follow up his answers with related questions

15. You are assigned to investigate a complaint of child neglect made against a minority mother by her non-minority neighbor. During an interview with you, the neighbor states that the mother allows her children to run around the streets half-dressed till late at night, and adds: *Of course, what can you expect from any of those people anyway?* Of the following, your *MOST* appropriate action is to

    15._____

    A. end the investigation, since the neighbor is clearly too prejudiced to be reliable

    B. tell the mother that the neighbor has made a complaint of child neglect against her

    C. seek evidence to support the complaint of child neglect made by the neighbor

    D. continue the interview with the neighbor in an attempt to get at the root of his prejudice against the mother

16. You are interviewing a couple with regard to available services for the husband's aged mother. During the interview, the husband casually mentions that he and his wife are thinking about becoming foster parents and would like to get some information on foster care programs offered through the department of social services. Of the following agencies within social services, the *MOST* appropriate one for you to refer this couple to is

    16._____

    A. family and adult services

    B. special services for children

    C. bureau of child support

    D. special services for adults

17. You have been helping one of your clients to obtain medical assistance for her two young children. Accidentally, you obtain evidence that the client may be involved in a criminal scheme to collect duplicate welfare checks at several different addresses. Of the following offices of the department of social services, the *MOST* appropriate one to which you should report this evidence is

    17._____

    A. the inspector general

    B. case intake and management

    C. the general counsel

    D. income support

Questions 18-25.

DIRECTIONS: Questions 18 through 25 are to be answered *SOLELY* on the basis of the
FACT SITUATION and REPORT FORM.

FACT SITUATION

On June 5, 2013, Mary Adams (Case No. ADC-2095732), lining at 1507 Montague Street, Apt. 3C, Brooklyn, New York, applied and was accepted for public assistance for herself and her three dependant children. Her husband, John, had left their home after an argument the previous week and had not returned, leaving Mrs. Adams without funds of any kind. She had tried to contact him at his place of employment, but was told that he had resigned several days prior to her call. When the Case Worker questioned Mrs. Adams about her husband's employment, income, and bank accounts, Mrs. Adams stated that he had done carpentry work during most of the years he had worked; his last known employer had been the Avco Lumber Company, 309 Amber Street, Queens, New York, where he had earned a weekly salary of $300. She then showed the Case Worker two bankbooks in her husband's name, which indicated a balance of $500 in one account and $275 in the other. A visit to Mr. Brown, a neighbor of the Adams', by the Case Worker, revealed that Mr. Adams had also told Mr. Brown about the existence of the bankbooks. A visit to the Avco Lumber Company by the Case Worker confirmed that Mr. Adams' gross salary had been $300 a week. This visit also revealed that Mr. Adams was a member of the Woodworkers' Union, Local #7, and that Mr. Adams' previous home address for the period from February '02 to June '08 was 1109 Wellington Street, Brooklyn, New York.

REPORT FORM

A.   CLIENT:

   1. Name:_____

   2. Address: _____

   3. Case No.: _____

   4. Acceptance Date:_____

   5. No. of Dependent Children: _____

B.   ABSENT PARENT:

   1. Name:_____

   2. Date of birth _____

   3. Place of Birth:_____

   4. Present Address: _____

   5. Regular Occupation: _____

   6. Union Affiliation: _____

   7. Name of Last Employer:_____

   8. Address of Last Employer: _____

   9.   a.   Weekly Earnings (Gross):_____
        b.   How Verified:_____

   10. a.   Weekly Earnings (Net): _____
        b.   How Verified:_____

   11. a.   Amount of Bank Accounts:_____
        b.   How Verified:_____

   12. Social Security No.:_____

   13. Last Known Home Address: _____

   14. Previous Addresses:_____

18. Based on the information given in the FACT SITUATION, the *MOST* appropriate of the   18.____
    following entries for item B.II.b is:

    A. *Revealed to Case Worker by Mrs. Adams*
    B. *Confirmed by visit to Mr. Brown*
    C. *Revealed by Woodworkers' Union, Local #7*
    D. *Confirmed by bankbooks shown by Mrs. Adams*

19. The *one* of the following which *BEST* answers item B.4 is: 19.____

    A. *unknown*
    B. *c/o Avco Lumber Company*
    C. *1109 Wellington Street, Brooklyn, New York*
    D. *1507 Montague Street, Brooklyn, New York*

20. Based on the information given in the FACT SITUATION, it is *NOT* possible to answer   20.____
    item

    A. A.2   B. A.5   C. B.6   D. B.10

21. The *one* of the following which would be *LEAST* helpful in tracing the missing parent is   21.____
    information found in item

    A. B.12   B. B.10.a   C. B.6   D. B.1

22. Based on the information given in the FACT SITUATION, it is *most likely* that the *SAME*   22.____
    entry would be made for items

    A. A.1 and B.1   B. A.4 and B.2
    C. B.9.a and B.10.a   D. A.2 and B.13

23. Based on the information in the FACT SITUATION, the entry : *1109 Wellington Street,*   23.____
    Brooklyn, New York would *most likely* be placed for item

    A. A.2   B. B.4   C. B.8   D. B.14

24. The *one* of the following items that can be answered based on the information given in   24.____
    the FACT SITUATION is

    A. B.2   B. B.3   C. B.9.b   D. B.12

25. Based on the information given in the FACT SITUATION, the figure *775* would appear in   25.____
    the entry for

    A. A.3   B. B.12   C. B.9.a   D. B.11.a

KEY (CORRECT ANSWERS)

1.	B		11.	A
2.	C		12.	C
3.	C		13.	B
4.	B		14.	D
5.	D		15.	C
6.	D		16.	B
7.	C		17.	A
8.	B		18.	D
9.	A		19.	A
10.	B		20.	D

21.	B
22.	D
23.	D
24.	C
25.	D

———

TEST 2

DIRECTIONS: Each question or incomplete statement is followed by several suggested answers or completions. Select the one that BEST answers the question or completes the statement. *PRINT THE LETTER OF THE CORRECT ANSWER IN THE SPACE AT THE RIGHT.*

1. A worker in a senior adult center is approached by one of his clients, an elderly man living alone and suffering from severe arthritis, who asks him how to go about obtaining homemaker services through the department of social services.
   Of the following, the *MOST* appropriate office of the department to which the worker should refer this client is:

   A. income support
   B. protective services for adults
   C. income maintenance
   D. case intake and management

1.____

2. Workers assigned to locate absent parents frequently ask various governmental agencies to search their records for information useful in determining the address of the person they are seeking.
   Of the following, the agency which is likely to be useful *most frequently* for this purpose is the

   A. motor vehicle bureau
   B. office of the district attorney
   C. department of investigation
   D. health and hospitals corporation

2.____

Questions 3-7.

DIRECTIONS: Questions 3 through 7 are to be answered *SOLELY* on the basis of the FACT SITUATION and PRELIMINARY INVESTIGATION FORM.

FACT SITUATION

COMPLAINT:

On March 1, Mrs. Mona Willard, a neighbor of the Smith family, reported to the Police Department that the Smith children, were being severely neglected, and she requested that an investigation be conducted. She based her complaint on the fact that, since the time three weeks ago when Janet Smith's husband, Charles, deserted Mrs. Smith and their two children, John, age 2, and Darlene, age 4, the children have been seen wandering in the neighborhood at all hours, inadequately dressed against the cold.

INVESTIGATION:

Investigation by the Police Department and the Department of Social Services revealed that the above charge was true and, further, that Mrs. Smith had inflicted cruel and harsh physical treatment upon the children in an attempt to discipline them. The children were immediately removed from their parent' s care and placed in a medical facility for tests and observation. It as found that the children were suffering from serious malnutrition and anemia and that they also showed signs of emotional disturbance.

CASE ACTION DECISION:

Conferences which you, the Case Worker, have held with Dr. Charles Jordan, a physician treating Mrs. Smith, and with Ellen Farraday, a psychiatric social worker from the Mental Health Consultation Center, confirm that Mrs. Smith is emotionally unstable at the present time and cannot care for her children. A written report from the Chief Resident Physician at the hospital where the children have been placed indicates that both children are presently doing well, but when released will need the security of an emotionally stable atmosphere. It has therefore been decided that placement in a foster he ia necessary for the children until such time as Mrs. Smith is judged to be capable of caring for them.

PRELIMINARY INVESTIGATION FORM

1. Child(ren) in Need of Protection :
      a. Name(s): _____
      b. Age (s) : _____

2. Alleged Perpetrator :
      a. Name: _____
      b. Relationship: _____

3. Present Status of Child(ren):
    ☐ a. Remaining with Subject Pending Investigation
    ☐ b. Removed to Relatives
    ☐ c. Removed to Foster Care
    ☐ d. In Hospital
    ☐ e. Other

4. Actions or Services Needed for Child(ren):
    ☐ a. Housekeeper
    ☐ b. Homemaker
    ☐ c. Day Care
    ☐ d. Home Attendant
    ☐ e. Relatives
    ☐ f. Foster Care

5. Contacts Made to Support Case Action Decision:

	I Phone	II Personal	III Written
a. Medical; School	☐	☐	☐
b. Relatives	☐	☐	☐
c. Social Agency	☐	☐	☐
d. Other	☐	☐	☐

3. The *one* of the following that should be entered in space 2.b is 　　　　3.____

    A. mother   B. father   C. neighbor   D. physician

4. The *one* of the following boxes that should be checked in item 3 is 　　　　4.____

    A. a   B. c   C. d   D. e

5. The *one* of the following boxes that should be checked in item 4 is 　　　　5.____

    A. a   B. c   C. d   D. f

6. Based on the information given in the FACT SITUATION, the boxes that should be 　　　　6.____
checked off in item 5 are:

    A. a-II, a-III, c-II   B. a-II, c-II, c-III
    C. a-I, a-II, a-III   D. b-II, c-I, c-II

7. The *one* of the following that would *CORRECTLY* appear as part of the entry to item 1.a 　　　　7.____
is

    A. Mona   B. Janet   C. Darlene   D. Ellen

Questions 8-12.

DIRECTIONS: Answer Questions 8 through 12 *SOLELY* on the basis of the information contained in the following passage:

It is desirable, whenever possible, to have long-term elderly patients return to their own
homes after hospitalization, provided that the medical condition is not acute. Of course, there
must be room for the patient; the family must be able to provide some necessary care; and a
physician's services must be available. Although the patient's family may be able to provide
most services for the patient in his own home, this is generally unlikely because of the nature
of the illness and the patient's need for a variety of services. Recently, hospital personnel,
public health workers, visiting nurse associations, and community leaders have been
developing home-care programs, which make the services of the hospital available to the
patient who is not ill enough to require the concentrated technical facilities of a general hospital, but who is unable to attend an outpatient clinic or a physician's office. These services are
those of the physician, visiting nurse, physical therapist, occupational therapist, social worker,
and homemaker, as needed. There is also provision for readmission to the hospital for specific purposes and return to home care.

8. According to the passage above, it would be *UNDESIRABLE* to have an elderly patient 　　　　8.____
return to his own home after hospitalization when the patient

    A. requires the services of a doctor
    B. may be in immediate danger due to his medical condition
    C. is under physical or occupational therapy
    D. cannot go to the outpatient clinic of the hospital

9. According to the passage above, the *services of the hospital* which are made available 　　　　9.____
by home-care programs include those of

    A. dietitians   B. visiting nurses
    C. public health administrators   D. community workers

10. The *one* of the following statements about home-care programs which is *BEST* supported by the paragraph above is that home-care programs   10.____

    A. have been developed in part by hospital personnel
    B. relieve workloads of hospital personnel
    C. decrease public expenditures for hospitalization of the elderly
    D. reduce readmissions of elderly patients to hospitals

11. According to the above passage, home-care programs would be *LEAST* likely to include   11.____
the services of a

    A. homemaker   B. social worker
    C. physician   D. hospital technician

12. It may be *inferred* from the passage above that a *MAJOR* purpose of home-care programs is to   12.____

    A. increase the demand for physicians, nurses, and other medical personnel
    B. provide patients in their homes with services similar to those provided in hospitals
    C. reduce the need for general hospitals and outpatient clinics
    D. relieve the family of their responsibility of caring for the patient

Questions 13-17.

DIRECTIONS: Answer Questions 13 through 17 *SOLELY* on the basis of the information contained in the following DUTIES STATEMENT.

DUTIES STATEMENT OF THE VIOLATION CENTER (VC) CASE WORKER

1. Receives telephone, mail, and in-person reports of suspected violations from mandated and non-mandated sources, as well as from the New York State Violation Bureau (NYSVB). Informs mandated sources that they must send a written summary of their report, on form DSS-555, within 48 hours, to the Central Office of VC, 265 Church Street, New York, N. Y.

2. Completes in-office portion of DSS-555 received from mandated sources as fully as possible. Checks that report summary is specific, factual, and detailed. (See NYSVB Instructions on page 213.)

3. When DSS-555 is received, clears Central Office of VC for any previous record of violation on file in Central Office. If record exists, enters additional information from file record on to DSS-555. Also requests Central Office Clerk to provide appropriate record number of previous record and enters additional information from file record on to DSS-555. Also requests Central Office Clerk to provide appropriate record number of previous record and enters it in correct box on form.

4. Determines appropriate Central Office Sex Code and Reporting Source Code for each violation. (The Codes are in the VC Manual.) The codes are then entered on the bottom of the reverse side of the DSS-555.

5. Determines appropriate Service Area Code for the address in the summary. The address is the location of the violation, if known. (If the location of the violation is unknown, the address of the primary witness shall be used.) Enters Service Area Code on reverse of DSS-555. All report summaries involving violations by N.Y.C. employees are sent to the Manhattan Borough Office of VC for clearance and transmittal to BEM.

13. According to the DUTIES STATEMENT above, when a report of a suspected violation is received, a written summary of their report on DSS-555 must be sent within 48 hours by   13.____

    A. mandated sources   B. non-mandated sources   C. the NYSVB
    D. mandated and non-mandated sources, as well as by the NYSVB

14. From the above DUTIES STATEMENT, it may be *inferred* that the Case Worker whose duties are described is *most likely* assigned to   14.____

    A. the Manhattan Borough Office of VC
    B. the New York State Violation Bureau
    C. the Central Office of VC
    D. BEM

15. According to the DUTIES STATEMENT above, the Central Office Sex Code is entered on the DSS-555   15.____

    A. on the opposite side from the Service Area Code
    B. on the front of the form
    C. above the Service Area Code on the form
    D. on the bottom of the back of the form

16. According to the above DUTIES STATEMENT, a Case Worker can determine the appropriate Reporting Source Code for a violation by consulting   16.____

    A. NYSVB Instructions   B. the Central Office Clerk
    C. the VC Manual   D. the Service Area Code

17. As used in paragraph 2 of the DUTIES STATEMENT above, the word *detailed* means, most nearly,   17.____

    A. fully descriptive   B. complicated
    C. of considerable length   D. well-written

Questions 18-25.

DIRECTIONS: Refer to the following SEMI-MONTHLY FAMILY ALLOWANCE SCHEDULE and CONVERSION TABLE when answering Questions 18 through 25.

FIGURE NO. 1

SEMI-MONTHLY FAMILY ALLOWANCE SCHEDULE FOR MAINTENANCE OF LEGALLY RESPONSIBLE RELATIVE AND DEPENDENTS, BASED UPON TOTAL NUMBER OF PERSONS IN PRESENT HOUSEHOLD. (ALL SURPLUS IS TO BE USED AS CONTRIBUTION TO RECIPIENTS OF PUBLIC ASSISTANCE.)

TOTAL NUMBER OF PERSONS IN PRESENT HOUSEHOLD	ONE	TWO	THREE	FOUR	FIVE	SIX	EACH ADDITIONAL PERSON
SEMI-MONTHLY FAMILY ALLOWANCE	$1600	$1915	$2200	$2605	$2800	$3205	$350

FIGURE NO. 2
CONVERSION TABLE - WEEKLY TO SEMI-MONTHLY AMOUNTS

DOLLARS

Weekly Amount	Semi-Monthly Amount	Weekly Amount	Semi-Monthly Amount
$10.00	$ 21.70	$510.00	$1105.00
20.00	43.30	520.00	1126.70
30.00	65.00	530.00	1148.30
40.00	86.70	540.00	1170.00
50.00	108.30	550.00	1191.70
60.00	130.00	560.00	1213.30
70.00	151.70	570.00	1235.00
80.00	173.30	580.00	1256.70
90.00	195.00	590.00	1278.30
100.00	216.70	600.00	1300.00
110.00	238.30	610.00	1321.70
120.00	260.00	620.00	1343.30
130.00	281.70	630.00	1365.00
140.00	303.30	640.00	1386.70
150.00	325.00	650.00	1408.30
160.00	346.70	660.00	1430.00
170.00	368.30	670.00	1451.70
180.00	390.00	680.00	1473.30
190.00	411.70	690.00	1495.00
200.00	433.30	700.00	1516.70
210.00	455.00	710.00	1538.30
220.00	476.70	720.00	1560.00
230.00	498.30	730.00	1581.70
240.00	520.00	740.00	1603.30
250.00	541.70	750.00	1625.00
260.00	563.30	760.00	1646.70
270.00	585.00	770.00	1668.30
280.00	606.70	780.00	1690.00
290.00	628.30	790.00	1711.70
300.00	650.00	800.00	1733.30
310.00	671.70	810.00	1755.00
320.00	693.30	820.00	1776.70
330.00	715.00	830.00	1798.30
340.00	736.70	840.00	1820.00
350.00	783.00	850.00	1841.70
360.00	780.00	860.00	1863.30
370.00	801.70	870.00	1885.00
380.00	823.30	880.00	1906.70
390.00	845.00	890.00	1928.30
400.00	866.70	900.00	1950.00
410.00	888.30	910.00	1971.70
420.00	910.00	920.00	1993.30
430.00	931.70	930.00	2015.00
440.00	953.30	940.00	2036.70
450.00	975.00	950.00	2058.30
460.00	996.70	960.00	2080.00
470.00	1018.30	970.00	2101.70
480.00	1040.00	980.00	2123.30
490.00	1061.70	990.00	2145.00
500.00	1083.30	1000.00	2166.70

CENTS

Weekly Amount	Semi-Monthly Amount	Weekly Amount	Semi-Monthly Amount
$0.10	$0.20	$5.10	$11.10
0.20	0.40	5.20	11.30
0.30	0.70	5.30	11.50
0.40	0.90	5.40	11.70
0.50	1.10	5.50	11.90
0.60	1.30	5.60	12.10
0.70	1.50	5.70	12.40
0.80	1.70	5.80	12.60
0.90	2.00	5.90	12.80
1.00	2.20	6.00	13.00
1.10	2.40	6.10	13.20
1.20	2.60	6.20	13.40
1.30	2.80	6.30	13.70
1.40	3.00	6.40	13.90
1.50	3.30	6.50	14.10
1.60	3.50	6.60	14.30
1.70	3.70	6.70	14.50
1.80	3.90	6.80	14.70
1.90	4.10	6.90	15.00
2.00	4.30	7.00	15.20
2.10	4.60	7.10	15.40
2.20	4.80	7.20	15.60
2.30	5.00	7.30	15.80
2.40	5.20	7.40	16.00
2.50	5.40	7.50	16.30
2.60	5.60	7.60	16.50
2.70	5.90	7.70	16.70
2.80	6.10	7.80	16.90
2.90	6.30	7.90	17.10
3.00	6.50	8.00	17.30
3.10	6.70	8.10	17.60
3.20	6.90	8.20	17.80
3.30	7.20	8.30	18.00
3.40	7.40	8.40	18.20
3.50	7.60	8.50	18.40
3.60	7.80	8.60	18.60
3.70	8.00	8.70	18.90
3.80	8.20	8.80	19.10
3.90	8.50	8.90	18.30
4.00	8.70	9.00	19.50
4.10	8.90	9.10	19.70
4.20	9.10	9.20	19.90
4.30	9.30	9.30	20.20
4.40	9.50	9.40	20.40
4.50	9.80	9.50	20.60
4.60	10.00	9.60	20.80
4.70	10.20	9.70	21.00
4.80	10.40	9.80	21.20
4.90	10.60	9.90	21.50
5.00	10.80		

DIRECTIONS: Questions 18 through 25 are to be answered *SOLELY* on the basis of the SEMI-MONTHLY FAMILY ALLOWANCE SCHEDULE FOR MAINTENANCE OF LEGALLY RESPONSIBLE RELATIVE (FIGURE NO. 1) and CONVERSION TABLE (FIGURE NO. 2) given on pages 5 and 6 and the information and case situations given below.

Questions 18 through 21 are based on Case Situation No. 1;
Questions 22 through 25 are based on Case Situation No. 2.

INFORMATION

Legally responsible relatives living apart from persons on public assistance are asked to contribute toward the support of these persons. The amount of contribution depends on several factors, such as the number of persons in the legally responsible relative's present household who are dependent on his income (including himself), the amount of his gross income, and his expenses incident to employment. Since his contribution is computed on a semi-monthly basis, all figures must be broken down into semi-monthly amounts. Weekly amounts can be converted into semi-monthly amounts by using the conversion table on page 6.

The amount of support is computed as follows:

1. Determine total weekly gross income (the wages or salary *before* payroll deductions) of legally responsible relative.
2. Deduct all weekly expenses incident to employment such as federal, state, and city income taxes, Social Security payments, State Disability Insurance payments, union dues, cost of transportation, and $10.00 maximum per work day for lunch.
3. Remaining income shall be considered as weekly net income of legally responsible relative.
4. Convert weekly net income to semi-monthly net income, using data in FIGURE NO. 2.
5. Semi-monthly net income is compared to the semi-monthly allowance (see FIGURE NO. 1). If there is an excess of net income, then that amount is considered available as the contribution to the public assistance household. If the semi-monthly allowance is greater than the semi-monthly net income, then there is an income deficit, and there is no income available as a contribution to the public assistance household.
6. The formula for computing the semi-monthly contribution is:

> Semi-Monthly Net Income
> - Semi-Monthly Family Allowance
> = Semi-Monthly Amount of Income Available Towards Contribution to Public Assistance Household

Case Situation No. 1

Mr. Andrew Young is separated from his wife and family and lives with one dependent in a 3-room furnished apartment. Mr. Young is employed as a dishwasher and his gross wages are $1000.00 per week. He is employed 5 days a week and spends $14.00 a day carfare. He spends $20.00 a work day on lunch. His weekly salary deductions are as follows:

Federal Income Tax	$142.30
State Income Tax	26.00
City Income Tax	9.80
Social Security	62.10
New York State Disability Insurance	5.30
Union Dues	5.00

Mr. Young's wife and two children, for whom he is legally responsible, are currently receiving public assistance.

Case Situation No. 2

Mr. Donald Wilson resides with six dependents in a seven-room unfurnished apartment. Mr. Wilson is employed as an automobile salesman and his gross wages are $4000.00 per week. He is employed five days a week and spends $10.00 a day carfare. He spends $50.00 a work day for lunch. His weekly salary deductions are as follows:

Federal Income Tax	$705.50
State Income Tax	150.00
City Income Tax	97.00
Social Security	301.00
New York State Disability Insurance	52.50
Union Dues	Not Union Member

Mr. Wilson is the only wage earner in his present household. His legal wife and minor child, for whom he is legally responsible, are both receiving public assistance.

NOTE: When answering Questions 18 through 21, refer to Case Situation No. 1.

18. The *weekly amount* that Mr. Young contributes toward Social Security, New York State Disability Insurance, Income Taxes, and Union Dues is, most nearly,

    A. $214.70   B. $250.50   C. $320.50   D. $370.50

18.____

19. The *total amount* of all weekly expenses incident to Mr. Young's employment which should be deducted from his weekly gross earnings, is, most nearly,

    A. $214.70   B. $250.50   C. $370.50   D. $420.50

19.____

20. *Which one* of the following amounts is Mr. Young's *semimonthly net income?*

    A. $1259.00   B. $1363.90   C. $1623.90   D. $1701.50

20.____

21. The *semi-monthly amount* of income available to the contribution to Mr. Young's wife and two children is, most nearly,

    A. $0.00   B. $23.90   C. $236.10   D. $551.10

21.____

NOTE: When answering Questions 22 through 25, refer to Case Situation No. 2.

22. The *weekly amount* that Mr. Wilson contributes toward Social Security, New York State Disability Insurance, Federal Income Tax, and Union Dues is, most nearly,

    A. $1059.00   B. $1159.00   C. $1306.00   D. $1406.00

22.____

23. The *total amount* of all weekly expenses incident to Mr. Wilson's employment, which should be deducted from his weekly gross earnings, is, most nearly,

    A. $1159.00   B. $1306.00   C. $1406.00   D. $1606.00

23.____

24. The *semi-monthly family allowance* for Mr. Wilson and his six dependents is, most nearly,

    A. $2594.00   B. $3205.00   C. $3555.00   D. $4000.00

24.____

25. The *semi-monthly amount* of Mr. Wilson's income available for contribution to his wife and child is, most nearly,

    A. $1633.00   B. $2065.40   C. $2594.00   D. $2810.20

25.____

KEY (CORRECT ANSWERS)

1.	D		11.	D
2.	A		12.	B
3.	A		13.	A
4.	C		14.	C
5.	D		15.	D
6.	A		16.	C
7.	C		17.	A
8.	B		18.	B
9.	B		19.	C
10.	A		20.	B

21.	A
22.	A
23.	C
24.	C
25.	B

———

INTERVIEWING
EXAMINATION SECTION
TEST 1

DIRECTIONS: Each question or incomplete statement is followed by several suggested answers or completions. Select the one that BEST answers the question or completes the statement. *PRINT THE LETTER OF THE CORRECT ANSWER IN THE SPACE AT THE RIGHT.*

1. Of the methods given below for obtaining desired information from applicants, the one considered the BEST interviewing method is to   1.____

    A. work from an outline, asking the questions in the order in which they appear and requiring the applicant to give specific answers
    B. let the applicant tell what he has to say in his own way first, the interviewer then taking responsibility for asking questions on points not covered
    C. tell the applicant all the facts that it is necessary to have, then letting him give the information in any way he chooses
    D. verify all such facts as birth date, income, and past employment before seeing the applicant, then asking the applicant to fill in the remaining gaps when he is inter-viewed

2. Suppose an applicant objects to answering a question regarding his recent employment and asks, "What business is it of yours, young man?"   2.____
In conducting the interview, the MOST constructive course of action for you to take under the circumstances would be to

    A. tell the applicant you have no intention of prying into his personal affairs and go on to the next question
    B. refer the applicant to your supervisor
    C. rephrase the question so that only a "Yes" or "No" answer is required
    D. explain why the question is being asked

3. An interview is BEST conducted in private PRIMARILY because   3.____

    A. the person interviewed will tend to be less self-conscious
    B. the interviewer will be able to maintain his continuity of thought better
    C. it will insure that the interview is "off the record"
    D. people tend to "show off" before an audience

4. An interviewer will be better able to understand the person interviewed and his problems if he recognizes that much of the person's behavior is due to *motives*   4.____

    A. which are deliberate   B. of which he is unaware
    C. which are inexplicable   D. which are kept under contrc

5. When an applicant is repeatedly told that "everything will be all right," the effect that can *usually* be expected is that he will   5.____

    A. develop overt negativistic reactions toward the agency
    B. become too closely identified with the interviewer
    C. doubt the interviewer's ability to understand and help with his problems
    D. have greater confidence in the interviewer

6. While interviewing a client, it is *preferable* that the interviewer   6.____

    A. take no notes in order to avoid disturbing the client
    B. focus primary attention on the client while the client is talking
    C. take no notes in order to impress upon the client the interviewer's ability to remember all the pertinent facts of his case
    D. record all the details in order to show the client that what he says is important

7. During an interview, a curious applicant asks several questions about the interviewer's   7.____
private life. As the interviewer, you should

    A. refuse to answer such questions
    B. answer his questions fully
    C. explain that your primary concern is with his problems and that discussion of your personal affairs will not be helpful in meeting his needs
    D. explain that it is the responsibility of the interviewer to ask questions and not to answer them

8. An interviewer can BEST establish a good relationship with the person being interviewed   8.____
by

    A. assuming casual interest in the statements made by the person being interviewed
    B. asking questions which enable the person to show pride in his knowledge
    C. taking the point of view of the person interviewed
    D. showing a genuine interest in the person

9. An interviewer's attention must be directed toward himself as well as toward the person   9.____
interviewed.
This statement *means* that the interviewer should

    A. keep in mind the extent to which his own prejudices may influence his judgment
    B. rationalize the statements made by the person interviewed
    C. gain the respect and confidence of the person interviewed
    D. avoid being too impersonal

10. *More* complete expression will be obtained from a person being interviewed if the inter-   10.____
viewer can create the impression that

    A. the data secured will become part of a permanent record
    B. official information must be accurate in every detail
    C. it is the duty of the person interviewed to give accurate data
    D. the person interviewed is participating in a discussion of his own problems

11. The practice of asking leading questions should be *avoided* in an interview because the   11.____

    A. interviewer risks revealing his attitudes to the person being interviewed
    B. interviewer may be led to ignore the objective attitudes of the person interviewed
    C. answers may be unwarrantedly influenced
    D. person interviewed will resent the attempt to lead him and will be less cooperative

12. A *good* technique for the interviewer to use in an effort to secure reliable data and to reduce the possibility of misunderstanding is to 12.____

    A. use casual undirected conversation, enabling the person being interviewed to talk about himself, and thus secure the desired information

    B. adopt the procedure of using direct questions regularly

    C. extract the desired information from the person being interviewed by putting him on the defensive

    D. explain to the person being interviewed the information desired and the reason for needing it

13. In interviewing an applicant, your attitude toward his veracity *should be* that the information he has furnished you is 13.____

    A. *untruthful* until you have had an opportunity to check the information

    B. *truthful* only insofar as verifiable facts are concerned

    C. *untruthful* because clients tend to interpret everything in their own favor

    D. *truthful* until you have information to the contrary

14. When an agency assigns its most experienced interviewers to conduct initial interviews with applicants, the MOST important reason for its action is that 14.____

    A. experienced workers are always older, and therefore, command the respect of applicants

    B. the applicant may be given a complete understanding of the procedures to be followed and the time involved in obtaining assistance

    C. applicants with fraudulent intentions will be detected, and prevented from obtaining further services from the agency

    D. the applicant may be given an understanding of the purpose of the assistance program and of the bases for granting assistance, in addition to the routine information

15. In conducting the *first* interview with an applicant, you should 15.____

    A. ask questions requiring "yes" or "no" answers in order to simplify the interview

    B. rephrase several of the key questions as a check on his previous statements

    C. let him tell his own story while keeping him to the relevant facts

    D. avoid showing any sympathy for the applicant while he is revealing his personal needs and problems

16. When an interviewer opens an interview by asking the client direct questions about his work, it is *very* likely that the client will feel 16.____

    A. that the interviewer is interested in him

    B. at ease if his work has been good

    C. free to discuss his attitudes toward his work

    D. that good reports are of great importance to the interviewer in his thinking

17. When an interviewer does NOT understand the meaning of a response that a client has made, the interviewer should 17.____

    A. proceed to another topic

    B. state that he does not understand and ask for clarification

    C. act as if he understands so that the client's confidence in him should not be shaken

    D. ask the client to rephrase his response

18. When an interviewer makes a response which brings on a high degree of resistance in the client, he should

    A. apologize and rephrase his remark in a less evocative manner
    B. accept the resistance on the part of the client
    C. ignore the client's resistance
    D. recognize that little more will be accomplished in the interview and suggest another appointment

18.____

19. *Most* definitions of interviewing would NOT include the following as a necessary aspect:

    A. The interviewer and client meet face-to-face and talk things out
    B. The client is experiencing considerable emotional disturbance
    C. A valuable learning opportunity is provided for the client
    D. The interviewer brings a special competence to the relationship

19.____

20. A powerful dynamic in the interviewing process and often the very *antonym* of its counterpart in the instructional process is

    A. encouraging accuracy
    B. emphasizing structure
    C. pointing up sequential and orderly thinking
    D. processing ambiguity and equivocation

20.____

21. Interviewing techniques are frequently useful in working with clients. A basic fundamental is an atmosphere which may BEST be described as

    A. non-threatening
    B. motivating for creativity
    C. highly charged to stimulate excitement
    D. fairly-well structured

21.____

22. In interviewing the disadvantaged client, the subtle technique of steering away from high-level educational and vocational plans must be *replaced* by

    A. a wait-and-see explanation to the client
    B. the use of prediction tables to determine possibilities and probabilities of overcoming this condition
    C. avoidance in discussing controversial issues of deprivation
    D. encouragement and concrete consideration for planning his future

22.____

23. The process of collecting, analyzing, synthesizing and interpreting information about the client should be

    A. completed prior to interviewing
    B. completed early in the interviewing process
    C. limited to a type of interviewing which is primarily diagnostic in purpose
    D. continuously pursued throughout interviewing

23.____

24. Catharsis, the "emotional unloading" of the client's feelings, has a value in the early stages of interviewing because it accomplishes all BUT which one of the following goals? It   24._____

    A.   relieves strong physiological tensions in the client
    B.   increases the client's axiety and aggrandizes his motivation to continue counseling
    C.   provides a strong substitute for "acting out" the client's aggressive feelings
    D.   releases emotional energy which the client has been using to bulwark his defenses

25. In the interviewing process, the interviewer should *usually* give information   25._____

    A.   whenever it is needed
    B.   at the end of the process
    C.   in the introductory interview
    D.   just before the client would ordinarily request it

KEY (CORRECT ANSWERS)

1.	B	11.	C
2.	D	12.	D
3.	A	13.	D
4.	B	14.	D
5.	C	15.	C
6.	B	16.	D
7.	C	17.	B
8.	D	18.	B
9.	A	19.	B
10.	D	20.	D

21.	A
22.	D
23.	D
24.	B
25.	A

TEST 2

DIRECTIONS: Each question or incomplete statement is followed by several suggested answers or completions. Select the one that BEST answers the question or completes the statement. *PRINT THE LETTER OF THE CORRECT ANSWER IN THE SPACE AT THE RIGHT.*

1. Of the following problems that might affect the conduct and outcome of an interview, the MOST troublesome and *usually* the MOST difficult for the interviewer to control is the

    A. tendency of the interviewee to anticipate the needs and preferences of the interviewer
    B. impulse to cut the interviewee off when he seems to have reached the end of an idea
    C. tendency of interviewee attitudes to bias the results
    D. tendency of the interviewer to do most of the talking

1.____

2. The supervisor *most likely* to be a good interviewer is one who

    A. is adept at manipulating people and circumstances toward his objective
    B. is able to put himself in the position of the interviewee
    C. gets the more difficult questions out of the way at the beginning of the interview
    D. develops one style and technique that can be used in any type of interview

2.____

3. A good interviewer guards against the tendency to form an overall opinion about an interviewee on the basis of a single aspect of the interviewee's makeup.
This statement refers to a well-known source of error in interviewing known as the

    A. assumption error   B. expectancy error
    C. extension effect   D. halo effect

3.____

4. In conducting an "exit interview" with an employee who is leaving voluntarily, the interview's MAIN objective should be to

    A. see that the employee leaves with a good opinion of the organization
    B. learn the true reasons for the employee's resignation
    C. find out if the employee would consider a transfer
    D. try to get the employee to remain on the job

4.____

5. During an interview, an interviewee unexpectedly discloses a relevant but embarrassing personal fact.
It would be BEST for the interviewer to

    A. listen calmly, avoiding any gesture or facial expression that would suggest approval or disapproval of what is related
    B. change the subject, since further discussion in this area may reveal other embarrassing, but irrelevant, personal facts
    C. apologize to the interviewee for having led him to reveal such a fact and promise not to do so again
    D. bring the interview to a close as quickly as possible in order to avoid a discussion which may be distressing to the interviewee

5.____

6. Suppose that, while you are interviewing an applicant for a position in your office, you notice a contradiction in facts in two of his responses.
For you to call the contradictions to his attention would be

    A. *inadvisable,* because it reduces the interviewee's level of participation
    B. *advisable,* because getting the facts is essential to a successful interview
    C. *inadvisable,* because the interviewer should use more subtle techniques to resolve any discrepancies
    D. *advisable,* because the interviewee should be impressed with the necessity for giving consistent answers

6._____

7. An interviewer should be aware that an *undesirable* result of including "leading questions" in an interview is to

    A. cause the interviewee to give "yes" or "no" answers with qualification or explanation
    B. encourage the interviewee to discuss irrelevant topics
    C. encourage the interviewee to give more meaningful information
    D. reduce the validity of the information obtained from the interviewee

7._____

8. The kind of interview which is *particularly* helpful in getting an employee to tell about his complaints and grievances is one in which

    A. a pattern has been worked out involving a sequence of exact questions to be asked
    B. the interviewee is expected to support his statements with specific evidence
    C. the interviewee is not made to answer specific questions but is encouraged to talk freely
    D. the interviewer has specific items on which he wishes to get or give information

8._____

9. Suppose you are scheduled to interview an employee under your supervision concerning a health problem. You know that some of the questions you will be asking him will seem embarrassing to him, and that he may resist answering these questions.
In general, to hold these questions for the *last* part of the interview would be

    A. *desirable;* the intervening time period gives the interviewer an opportunity to plan how to ask these sensitive questions
    B. *undesirable;* the employee will probably feel that he has been tricked when he suddenly must answer embarrassing questions
    C. *desirable;* the employee will probably have increased confidence in the interviewer and be more willing to answer these questions
    D. *undesirable;* questions that are important should not be deferred until the end of the interview

9._____

10. In conducting an interview, the BEST types of questions with which to begin the interview are those which the person interviewed is

    A. willing and able to answer
    B. willing but unable to answer
    C. able to but unwilling to answer
    D. unable and unwilling to answer

10._____

11. In order to determine accurately a child's age, it is BEST for an interviewer to rely on   11.____

    A. the child's grade in school   B. what the mother says
    C. birth records   D. a library card

12. In his first interview with a new employee, it would be LEAST appropriate for a unit super-   12.____
visor to

    A. find out the employee's preference for the several types of jobs to which he is able to assign him
    B. determine whether the employee will make good promotion material
    C. inform the employee of what his basic job responsibilities will be
    D. inquire about the employee's education and previous employment

13. If an interviewer takes care to phrase his questions carefully and precisely, the result will   13.____
most probably be that

    A. he will be able to determine whether the person interviewed is being truthful
    B. the free flow of the interview will be lost
    C. he will get the information he wants
    D. he will ask stereotyped questions and narrow the scope of the interview

14. When, during an interview, is the person interviewed LEAST likely to be cautious about   14.____
what he tells the interviewer?

    A. Shortly after the beginning when the questions normally suggest pleasant associations to the person interviewed
    B. As long as the interviewer keeps his questions to the point
    C. At the point where the person interviewed gains a clear insight into the area being discussed
    D. When the interview appears formally ended and goodbyes are being said

15. In an interview held for the purpose of getting information from the person interviewed, it   15.____
is sometimes desirable for the interviewer to repeat the answer he has received to a
question.
For the interviewer to rephrase such an answer in his *own* words is good practice
MAINLY because it

    A. gives the interviewer time to make up his next question
    B. gives the person interviewed a chance to correct any possible misunderstanding
    C. gives the person interviewed the feeling that the interviewer considers his answer important
    D. prevents the person interviewed from changing his answer

16. There are several methods of formulating questions during an interview. The particular   16.____
method used should be adapted to the interview problems presented by the person
being questioned.
Of the following methods of formulating questions during an interview, the *acceptable*
one is for the interviewer to ask questions which

    A. incorporate several items in order to allow a cooperative interviewee freedom to organize his statements
    B. are ambiguous in order to foil a distrustful interviewee

C. suggest the correct answer in order to assist an interviewee who appears confused
D. would help an otherwise unresponsive interviewee to become more responsive

17. For an interviewer to permit the person being interviewed to read the data the interviewer writes as he records the person's responses on a routine departmental form,is   17.____

    A. *desirable,* because it serves to assure the person interviewed that his responses are being recorded accurately
    B. *undesirable,* because it prevents the interviewer from clarifying uncertain points by asking additional questions
    C. *desirable,* because it makes the time that the person interviewed must wait while the answer is written seem shorter
    D. *undesirable,* because it destroys the confidentiality of the interview

18. Of the following methods of conducting an interview, the BEST is to   18.____

    A. ask questions with "yes" or "no" answers
    B. listen carefully and ask only questions that are pertinent
    C. fire questions at the interviewee so that he must answer sincerely and briefly
    D. read standardized questions to the person being interviewed

---

KEY (CORRECT ANSWERS)

1.	A	11.	C
2.	B	12.	B
3.	D	13.	C
4.	B	14.	D
5.	A	15.	B
6.	B	16.	D
7.	D	17.	A
8.	C	18.	B
9.	C		
10.	A		

INTERVIEWING
EXAMINATION SECTION
TEST 1

DIRECTIONS: Each question or incomplete statement is followed by several suggested answers or completions. Select the one that BEST answers the question or completes the statement. *PRINT THE LETTER OF THE CORRECT ANSWER IN THE SPACE AT THE RIGHT.*

1. An interview is BEST conducted in private primarily because   1.____

    A. the person interviewed will tend to be less self-conscious
    B. the interviewer will be able to maintain his continuity of thought better
    C. it will insure that the interview is "off the record"
    D. people tend to "show off" before an audience

2. An interviewer can BEST establish a good relationship with the person being interviewed by   2.____

    A. assuming casual interest in the statements made by the person being interviewed
    B. taking the point of view of the person interviewed
    C. controlling the interview to a major extent
    D. showing a genuine interest in the person

3. An interviewer will be better able to understand the person interviewed and his problems if he recognizes that much of the person's behavior is due to motives   3.____

    A. which are deliberate
    B. of which he is unaware
    C. which are inexplicable
    D. which are kept under control

4. An interviewer's attention must be directed toward himself as well as toward the person interviewed. This statement means that the interviewer should   4.____

    A. keep in mind the extent to which his own prejudices may influence his judgment
    B. rationalize the statements made by the person interviewed
    C. gain the respect and confidence of the person interviewed
    D. avoid being too impersonal

5. More complete expression will be obtained from a person being interviewed if the interviewer can create the impression that   5.____

    A. the data secured will become part of a permanent record
    B. official information must be accurate in every detail
    C. it is the duty of the person interviewed to give accurate data
    D. the person interviewed is participating in a discussion of his own problems

6. The practice of asking leading questions should be avoided in an interview because the   6.____

    A. interviewer risks revealing his attitudes to the person being interviewed
    B. interviewer may be led to ignore the objective attitudes of the person interviewed
    C. answers may be unwarrantedly influenced
    D. person interviewed will resent the attempt to lead him and will be less cooperative

7. A good technique for the interviewer to use in an effort to secure reliable data and to reduce the possibility of misunderstanding is to

    A. use casual undirected conversation, enabling the person being interviewed to talk about himself, and thus secure the desired information
    B. adopt the procedure of using direct questions regularly
    C. extract the desired information from the person being interviewed by putting him on the defensive
    D. explain to the person being interviewed the information desired and the reason for needing it

7.____

8. You are interviewing a patient to determine whether she is eligible for medical assistance. Of the many questions that you have to ask her, some are routine questions that patients tend to answer willingly and easily. Other questions are more personal and some patients tend to resent being asked them and avoid answering them directly. For you to begin the interview with the more personal questions would be

    A. *desirable,* because the end of the interview will go smoothly and the patient will be left with a warm feeling
    B. *undesirable,* because the patient might not know the answers to the questions
    C. *desirable,* because you will be able to return to these questions later to verify the accuracy of the responses
    D. *undesirable,* because you might antagonize the patient before you have had a chance to establish rapport

8.____

9. While interviewing a patient about her family composition, the patient asks you whether you are married.
Of the following, the MOST appropriate way for you to handle this situation is to

    A. answer the question briefly and redirect her back to the topic under discussion
    B. refrain from answering the question and proceed with the interview
    C. advise the patient that it is more important that she answer your questions than that you answer hers, and proceed with the interview
    D. promise the patient that you will answer her question later, in the hope that she will forget, and redirect her back to the topic under discussion

9.____

10. In response to a question about his employment history, a patient you are interviewing rambles and talks about unrelated matters.
Of the following, the MOST appropriate course of action for you to take FIRST is to

    A. ask questions to direct the patient back to his employment history
    B. advise him to concentrate on your questions and not to discuss irrelevant information
    C. ask him why he is resisting a discussion of his employment history
    D. advise him that if you cannot get the information you need, he will not be eligible for medical assistance

10.____

11. Suppose that a person you are interviewing becomes angry at some of the questions   11.____
you have asked, calls you meddlesome and nosy, and states that she will not answer
those questions.
Of the following, which is the BEST action for you to take?

    A. Explain the reasons the questions are asked and the importance of the answers.
    B. Inform the interviewee that you are only doing your job and advise her that she
       should answer your questions or leave the office.
    C. Report to your supervisor what the interviewee called you and refuse to continue
       the interview.
    D. End the interview and tell the interviewee she will not be serviced by your depart-
       ment.

12. Suppose that during the course of an interview the interviewee demands in a very rude   12.____
way that she be permitted to talk to your supervisor or someone in charge.
Which of the following is probably the BEST way to handle this situation?

    A. Inform your supervisor of the demand and ask her to speak to the interviewee.
    B. Pay no attention to the demands of the interviewee and continue the interview.
    C. Report to your supervisor and tell her to get another interviewer for this inter-
       viewee.
    D. Tell her you are the one "in charge" and that she should talk to you.

13. Of the following, the outcome of an interview by an aide depends MOST heavily on the   13.____

    A. personality of the interviewee
    B. personality of the aide
    C. subject matter of the questions asked
    D. interaction between aide and interviewee

14. Some patients being interviewed are primarily interested in making a favorable impres-   14.____
sion. The aide should be aware of the fact that such patients are more likely than other
patients to

    A. try to anticipate the answers the interviewer is looking for
    B. answer all questions openly and frankly
    C. try to assume the role of interviewer
    D. be anxious to get the interview over as quickly as possible

15. The type of interview which an aide usually conducts is substantially different from most   15.____
interviewing situations in all of the following aspects EXCEPT the

    A. setting   B. kinds of clients
    C. techniques employed   D. kinds of problems

16. During an interview, an aide uses a "leading question." This type of question is so-called   16.____
because it generally

    A. starts a series of questions about one topic
    B. suggests the answer which the aide wants
    C. forms the basis for a following "trick" question
    D. sets, at the beginning, the tone of the interview

17. Casework interviewing is always directed to the client and his situation. The one of the following which is the MOST accurate statement with respect to the proper focus of an interview is that the

    A. caseworker limits the client to concentration on objective data
    B. client is generally permitted to talk about facts and feelings with no direction from the caseworker
    C. main focus in casework interviews is on feelings rather than facts
    D. caseworker is responsible for helping the client focus on any material which seems to be related to his problems or difficulties

17.____

18. Assume that you are conducting a training program for the caseworkers under your supervision. At one of the sessions, you discuss the problem of interviewing a dull and stupid client who gives a slow and disconnected case history. The BEST of the following interviewing methods for you to recommend in such a case in order to ascertain the facts is for the caseworker to

    A. ask the client leading questions requiring "yes" or "no" answers
    B. request the client to limit his narration to the essential facts so that the interview can be kept as brief as possible
    C. review the story with the client, patiently asking simple questions
    D. tell the client that unless he is more cooperative he cannot be helped to solve his problem

18.____

19. A recent development in casework interviewing procedure, known as multiple-client interviewing, consists of interviews of the entire family at the same time. However, this may not be an effective casework method in certain situations. Of the following, the situation in which the standard individual interview would be preferable is when

    A. family members derive consistent and major gratification from assisting each other in their destructive responses
    B. there is a crucial family conflict to which the members are reacting
    C. the family is overwhelmed by interpersonal anxieties which have not been explored
    D. the worker wants to determine the pattern of family interaction to further his diagnostic understanding

19.____

20. A follow-up interview was arranged for an applicant in order that he could furnish certain requested evidence. At this follow-up interview, the applicant still fails to furnish the necessary evidence. It would be MOST advisable for you to

    A. advise the applicant that he is now considered ineligible
    B. ask the applicant how soon he can get the necessary evidence and set a date for another interview
    C. question the applicant carefully and thoroughly to determine if he has misrepresented or falsified any information
    D. set a date for another interview and tell the applicant to get the necessary evidence by that time.

20.____

KEY (CORRECT ANSWERS)

1.	A	11.	A
2.	D	12.	A
3.	B	13.	D
4.	A	14.	A
5.	D	15.	C
6.	C	16.	B
7.	D	17.	D
8.	D	18.	C
9.	A	19.	A
10.	A	20.	B

TEST 2

DIRECTIONS: Each question or incomplete statement is followed by several suggested answers or completions. Select the one that BEST answers the question or completes the statement. *PRINT THE LETTER OF THE CORRECT ANSWER IN THE SPACE AT THE RIGHT.*

1. In interviewing, the practice of anticipating an applicant's answers to questions is generally

   A. *desirable,* because it is effective and economical when it is necessary to interview large numbers of applicants
   B. *desirable,* because many applicants have language difficulties
   C. *undesirable,* because it is the inalienable right of every person to answer as he sees fit
   D. *undesirable,* because applicants may tend to agree with the answer proposed by the interviewer even when the answer is not entirely correct

1.____

2. When an initial interview is being conducted, one way of starting is to explain the purpose of the interview to the applicant. The practice of starting the interview with such an explanation is generally

   A. *desirable,* because the applicant can then understand why the interview is necessary and what will be accomplished by it
   B. *desirable,* because it creates the rapport which is necessary to successful interviewing
   C. *undesirable,* because time will be saved by starting directly with the questions which must be asked
   D. *undesirable,* because the interviewer should have the choice of starting an interview in any manner he prefers

2.____

3. For you to use responses such as "That's interesting," "Uh-huh" and "Good" during an interview with a patient is

   A. *desirable,* because they indicate that the investigator is attentive
   B. *undesirable,* because they are meaningless to the patient
   C. *desirable,* because the investigator is not supposed to talk excessively
   D. *undesirable,* because they tend to encourage the patient to speak freely

3.____

4. During the course of a routine interview, the BEST tone of voice for an interviewer to use is

   A. authoritative   B. uncertain
   C. formal   D. conversational

4.____

5. It is recommended that interviews which inquire into the personal background of an individual should be held in private. The BEST reason for this practice is that privacy

   A. allows the individual to talk freely about the details of his background
   B. induces contemplative thought on the part of the interviewed individual
   C. prevents any interruptions by departmental personnel during the interview
   D. most closely resembles the atmosphere of the individual's personal life

5.____

6. Assume that you are interviewing a patient to determine whether he has any savings accounts. To obtain this information, the MOST effective way to phrase your question would be:

    A. "You don't have any savings, do you?"
    B. "At which bank do you have a savings account?"
    C. "Do you have a savings account?"
    D. "May I assume that you have a savings account?"

6._____

7. You are interviewing a patient who is not cooperating to the extent necessary to get all required information. Therefore, you decide to be more forceful in your approach.
In this situation, such a course of action is

    A. *advisable,* because such a change in approach may help to increase the patient's participation
    B. *advisable,* because you will be using your authority more effectively
    C. *inadvisable,* because you will not be able to change this approach if it doesn't produce results
    D. *inadvisable,* because an aggressive approach generally reduces the validity of the interview

7._____

8. You have attempted to interview a patient on two separate occasions, and both attempts were unsuccessful. The patient has been totally uncooperative and you sense a personal hostility toward you.
Of the following, the BEST way to handle this type of situation would be to

    A. speak to the patient in a courteous manner and ask him to explain exactly what he dislikes about you
    B. inform the patient that you will not allow personality conflicts to disrupt the interview
    C. make no further attempt to interview the patient and recommend that he be billed in full
    D. discuss the problem with your supervisor and suggest that another investigator be assigned to try to interview the patient

8._____

9. At the beginning of an interview, a patient with normal vision tells you that he is reluctant to discuss his finances. You realize that it will be necessary in this case to ask detailed questions about his net income. When you begin this line of questioning, of the following, the LEAST important aspect you should consider is your

    A. precise wording of the question
    B. manner of questioning
    C. tone of voice
    D. facial expressions

9._____

10. A caseworker under your supervision has been assigned the task of interviewing a man who is applying for foster home placement for his two children. The caseworker seeks your advice as to how to question this man, stating that she finds the applicant to be a timid and self-conscious person who seems torn between the necessity of having to answer the worker's questions truthfully and the effect he thinks his answers will have on his application. Of the following, the BEST method for the caseworker to use in order to determine the essential facts in this case is to

10._____

A. assure the applicant that he need not worry since the majority of applications for foster home placement are approved
B. delay the applicant's narration of the facts important to the case until his embarrassment and fears have been overcome
C. ignore the statements made by the applicant and obtain all the required information from his friends and relatives
D. inform the applicant that all statements made by him will be verified and are subject to the law governing perjury

11. Assume that a worker is interviewing a boy in his assigned group in order to help him find a job. At the BEGINNING of the interview, the worker should   11.____

A. suggest a possible job for the youth
B. refer the youth to an employment agency
C. discuss the youth's work history and skills with him
D. refer the youth to the manpower and career development agency

12. As part of the investigation to locate an absent father, you make a field visit to interview one of the father's friends. Before beginning the interview, you identify yourself to the friend and show him your official identification.
For you to do this is, generally,   12.____

A. *good practice,* because the friend will have proof that you are authorized to make such confidential investigations
B. *poor practice,* because the friend may not answer your questions when he knows why you are interviewing him
C. *good practice,* because your supervisor can confirm from the friend that you actually made the interview
D. *poor practice,* because the friend may warn the absent father that your agency is looking for him

13. You are interviewing a client in his home as part of your investigation of an anonymous complaint that he has been receiving Medicaid fraudulently. During the interview, the client frequently interrupts your questions to discuss the hardships of his life and the bitterness he feels about his medical condition.
Of the following, the BEST way for you to deal with these discussions is to   13.____

A. cut them off abruptly, since the client is probably just trying to avoid answering your questions
B. listen patiently, since these discussions may be helpful to the client and may give you information for your investigation
C. remind the client that you are investigating a complaint against him and he must answer directly
D. seek to gain the client's confidence by discussing any personal or medical problems which you yourself may have

14. While interviewing an absent father to determine his ability to pay child support, you realize that his answers to some of your questions contradict his answers to other questions.
Of the following, the BEST way for you to try to get accurate information from the father is to   14.____

A. confront him with his contradictory answers and demand an explanation from him

B. use your best judgment as to which of his answers are accurate and question him accordingly

C. tell him that he has misunderstood your questions and that he must clarify his answers

D. ask him the same questions in different words and follow up his answers with related questions

15. Assume that an applicant, obviously under a great deal of stress, talks continuously and rambles, making it difficult for you to determine the exact problem and her need. In order to make the interview more successful, it would be BEST for you to

    15.____

A. interrupt the applicant and ask her specific questions in order to get the information you need

B. tell the applicant that her rambling may be a basic cause of her problem

C. let the applicant continue talking as long as she wishes

D. ask the applicant to get to the point because other people are waiting for you

16. A worker must be able to interview clients all day and still be able to listen and maintain interest.
Of the following, it is MOST important for you to show interest in the client because, if you appear interested,

    16.____

A. the client is more likely to appreciate your professional status

B. the client is more likely to disclose a greater amount of information

C. the client is less likely to tell lies

D. you are more likely to gain your supervisor's approval

17. When you are interviewing clients, it is important to notice and record how they say what they say—angrily, nervously, or with "body English"—because these signs may

    17.____

A. tell you that the client's words are the opposite of what the client feels and you may need to dig to find out what those feelings are

B. be the prelude to violent behavior which no aide is prepared to handle

C. show that the client does not really deserve serious consideration

D. be important later should you be asked to defend what you did for the client

18. The patient you are interviewing is reticent and guarded in responding to your questions. He is not providing the information needed to complete his application for medical assistance.
In this situation, the one of the following which is the most appropriate course of action for you to take FIRST is to

    18.____

A. end the interview and ask him to contact you when he is ready to answer your questions

B. advise the patient that you cannot end the interview until he has provided all the information you need to complete the application

C. emphasize to the patient the importance of the questions and the need to answer them in order to complete the application

D. advise the patient that if he answers your questions the interview will be easier for both of you

19. At the end of an interview with a patient, he describes a problem he is having with his   19.____
teenage son, who is often truant and may be using narcotics. The patient asks you for
advice in handling his son.
Of the following, the MOST appropriate action for you to take is to

    A. make an appointment to see the patient and his son together
    B. give the patient a list of drug counseling programs to which he may refer his son
    C. suggest to the patient that his immediate concern should be his own hospitalization
       rather than his son's problem
    D. tell the patient that you are not qualified to assist him but will attempt to find out
       who can

20. A MOST appropriate condition in the use of direct questions to obtain personal data in an   20.____
interview is that, whenever possible,

    A. the direct questions be used only as a means of encouraging the person inter-
       viewed to talk about himself
    B. provision be made for recording the information
    C. the direct questions be used only after all other methods have failed
    D. the person being interviewed understands the reason for requesting the informa-
       tion

––––––––

KEY (CORRECT ANSWERS)

1.	D	11.	C
2.	A	12.	A
3.	A	13.	B
4.	D	14.	D
5.	A	15.	A
6.	B	16.	B
7.	A	17.	A
8.	D	18.	C
9.	A	19.	D
10.	B	20.	D

––––––––

READING COMPREHENSION
UNDERSTANDING AND INTERPRETING WRITTEN MATERIAL

EXAMINATION SECTION
TEST 1

DIRECTIONS: Each question or incomplete statement is followed by several suggested answers or completions. Select the one that BEST answers the question or completes the statement. *PRINT THE LETTER OF THE CORRECT ANSWER IN THE SPACE AT THE RIGHT.*

Questions 1-2.

DIRECTIONS: Questions 1 and 2 are to be answered SOLELY on the basis of the following passage.

The new suburbia that is currently being built does not look much different from the old; there has, however, been an increase in the class and race polarization that has been developing between the suburbs and the cities for several generations now. The suburbs have become the home for an ever larger proportion of working-class, middle-class, and upper-class whites; the cities, for an even larger proportion of poor and non-white people. A great number of cities are 30 to 50 percent non-white in population, with more and larger ghettos than cities have ever had. Now, there is greater urban poverty on the one hand, and stronger suburban opposition to open housing and related policies to solve the cities' problems on the other hand. The urban crisis will worsen; and although there is no shortage of rational solutions, nothing much will be done about the crisis unless white America permits a radical change of public policy and undergoes a miraculous change of attitude towards its cities and their populations.

1.   Which of the following statements is IMPLIED by the above passage?   1.____

    A.   The percentage of non-whites in the suburbs is increasing.
    B.   The policies of suburbanites have contributed to the seriousness of the urban crisis.
    C.   The problems of the cities defy rational solutions.
    D.   There has been a radical change in the appearance of both suburbia and the cities in the past few years.

2.   Of the following, the title which BEST describes the passage's main theme is: 2.____

    A.   THE NEW SUBURBIA
    B.   URBAN POVERTY
    C.   URBAN-SUBURBAN POLARIZATION
    D.   WHY AMERICANS WANT TO LIVE IN THE SUBURBS

Questions 3-4.

DIRECTIONS: Questions 3 and 4 are to be answered selecting the BEST interpretation of the following paragraph.

One of the most familiar *type* dichotomies is Jung's introvert versus extrovert. Introverts are motivated by principles, extroverts by expediency; introverts are thinkers, extroverts are doers; and so on. Analysis of the way people react to principle versus expediency situations, however, has demonstrated that most people would have to be described as ambiverts (i.e., they exhibit both introverted and extroverted behavior depending upon the specific situation). Of course, some people behave in a more introverted way than others. A graphic representation of the number of persons exhibiting various degrees of such behavior along a continuum would approximate the familiar bell-shaped curve.

3.   A.   Extreme extroverts exhibit deviant behavior.   3.____
      B.   The bell-shaped curve would indicate that there are slightly more
           introverts than extroverts.
      C.   A continuum is used to determine whether a person is an introvert
           or an extrovert.
      D.   There is really very little difference between an introvert, an extro-
           vert, or an ambivert.

4.   A.   Extroverts are not thinkers, and introverts are not doers.   4.____
      B.   Ambiverts *think* more than they *do.*
      C.   Ambiverts outnumber introverts in the general society.
      D.   Extroverts possess fewer principles than introverts.

5.   The fundamental desires for food, shelter, family, and approval, and their accompanying   5.____
      instinctive forms of behavior, are among the most important forces in human life because
      they are essential to and directly connected with the preservation and the welfare of the
      individual as well as of the race.
      According to this statement,

      A.   as long as human beings are permitted to act instinctively, they will act wisely
      B.   the instinct for self-preservation makes the individual consider his own welfare
           rather than that of others
      C.   racial and individual welfare depend upon the fundamental desires
      D.   the preservation of the race demands that instinctive behavior be modified

6.   The growth of our cities, the increasing tendency to move from one part of the country to   6.____
      another, the existence of people of different cultures in the neighborhood, have together
      made it more and more difficult to secure group recreation as part of informal family and
      neighborhood life.
      According to this statement,

      A.   the breaking up of family and neighborhood ties discourages new family and neigh-
           borhood group recreation
      B.   neighborhood recreation no longer forms a significant part of the larger community
      C.   the growth of cities crowds out the development of all recreational activities
      D.   the non-English-speaking people do not accept new activities easily

7.   Sublimation consists in directing some inner urge, arising from a lower psychological   7.____
      level into some channel of interest on a higher psychological level. Pugnaciousness, for
      example, is directed into some athletic activity involving combat, such as football or box-
      ing, where rules of fair play and the ethics of the game lift the destructive urge for combat
      into a constructive experience and offer opportunities for the development of character
      and personality.

According to this statement,

    A. the manner of self-expression may be directed into constructive activities
    B. athletic activities such as football and boxing are destructive of character
    C. all conscious behavior on high psychological levels indicates the process of sublimation
    D. the rules of fair play are inconsistent with pugnaciousness

Questions 8-9.

DIRECTIONS: Questions 8 and 9 are to be answered on the basis of the following passage.

Just why some individuals choose one way of adjusting to their difficulties and others choose other ways is not known. Yet what an individual does when he is thwarted remains a reasonably good key to the understanding of his personality. If his responses to thwart-ings are emotional explosions and irrational excuses, he is tending to live in an unreal world. He may need help to regain the world of reality, the cause-and-effect world recognized by generations of thinkers and scientists. Perhaps he needs encouragement to redouble his efforts. Perhaps, on the other hand, he is striving for the impossible and needs to substitute a worthwhile activity within the range of his abilities. It is the part of wisdom to learn the nature of the world and of oneself in relation to it and to meet each situation as intelligently and as adequately as one can.

8.   The title that BEST expresses the idea of this paragraph is   8.____

    A. ADJUSTING TO LIFE
    B. ESCAPE FROM REALITY
    C. THE IMPORTANCE OF PERSONALITY
    D. EMOTIONAL CONTROL

9.   The writer argues that all should   9.____

    A. substitute new activities for old
    B. redouble their efforts
    C. analyze their relation to the world
    D. seek encouragement from others

Questions 10-15.

DIRECTIONS: Questions 10 through 15 are to be answered SOLELY on the basis of the information given in the paragraph below.

The use of role-playing as a training technique was developed during the past decade by social scientists, particularly psychologists, who have been active in training experiments. Originally, this technique was applied by clinical psychologists who discovered that a patient appears to gain understanding of an emotionally disturbing situation when encouraged to act out roles in that situation. As applied in government and business organizations, the purpose of role-playing is to aid employees to understand certain work problems involving interpersonal relations and to enable observers to evaluate various reactions to them. Thus, for example, on the problem of handling grievances, two individuals from the group might be selected to act out extemporaneously the parts of subordinate and supervisor. When this situation is enacted by various pairs among the class and the techniques and results are discussed, the members of the group are presumed to reach conclusions about the most effective means of handling similar situations. Often the use of role reversal, where participants take parts different from their actual work roles, assists individuals to gain more insight into other people's problems and viewpoints. Although role-playing can be a rewarding training device, the trainer must be aware of his responsibilities. If this technique is to be successful, thorough briefing of both actors and observers as to the situation in question, the participants' roles, and what to look for, is essential.

10. The role-playing technique was FIRST used for the purpose of   10.____

    A. measuring the effectiveness of training programs
    B. training supervisors in business organizations
    C. treating emotionally disturbed patients
    D. handling employee grievances

11. When role-playing is used in private business as a training device, the CHIEF aim is to   11.____

    A. develop better relations between supervisor and subordinate in the handling of grievances
    B. come up with a solution to a specific problem that has arisen
    C. determine the training needs of the group
    D. increase employee understanding of the human relation factors in work situations

12. From the above passage, it is MOST reasonable to conclude that when role-playing is used, it is preferable to have the roles acted out by   12.____

    A. only one set of actors
    B. no more than two sets of actors
    C. several different sets of actors
    D. the trainer or trainers of the group

13. Based on the above passage, a trainer using the technique of role reversal in a problem of first-line supervision should assign a senior enforcement agent to play the part of a(n)   13.____

    A. enforcement agent
    B. senior enforcement agent
    C. principal enforcement agent
    D. angry citizen

14. It can be inferred from the above passage that a *limitation* of role-play as a training method is that   14.____

    A. many work situations do not lend themselves to role-play
    B. employees are not experienced enough as actors to play the roles realistically
    C. only trainers who have psychological training can use it successfully
    D. participants who are observing and not acting do not benefit from it

15. To obtain good results from the use of role-play in training, a trainer should give participants   15.____

    A. a minimum of information about the situation so that they can act spontaneously
    B. scripts which illustrate the best method for handling the situation
    C. a complete explanation of the problem and the roles to be acted out
    D. a summary of work problems which involve interpersonal relations

Questions 16-20.

DIRECTIONS: Questions 16 through 20 are to be answered SOLELY on the basis of the following passage.

The dynamics of group behavior may be summed up by saying that the individuals in a group respond to many lines of force arising out of their relationship with every other member of a group and with the group itself. In addition, each member of a group quite naturally brings with him all the things that have been *bugging* him. Then, the situation or the setting in which the group meets, as well as the circumstances related to the formation of the group, are active working forces exerting some X influence upon each member of the group. Lastly, all of this kinetic energy is at the control of the person seeking to lead the group into some kind of action. If he is to produce something meaningful with the members of a group, he must utilize this energy, contain it, dissipate it in some fashion, or be faced with difficulty.

This dynamic force inherent in any group can be harnessed by a supervisor with leadership qualities, but it must be controlled. It will not be contained by acting without consultation with group members, by refusing to accept suggestions coming from the group, or by refusing to explain or even give notice of contemplated actions. However, it can be controlled by placing the focus upon the members of the group, rather than upon the supervisor, and depending upon the leader-supervisor to provide as many participative experiences for group members as is commensurate with his own decision-making responsibilities. It is true that this is subordinate-centered leadership, but the supervisor can gain strength through permissive leadership without sacrificing basic responsibilities for effective planning and adequate control of operations.

16. Of the following titles, the one that MOST closely describes the reading selection is   16.____

    A. THE SUPERVISOR WITH DYNAMIC LEADERSHIP POTENTIAL
    B. DISSIPATION OF GROUP ENERGY
    C. CONTROLLING GROUP RELATIONSHIPS
    D. SACRIFICING BASIC RESPONSIBILITIES

17. According to the above passage, the setting in which the group meets   17.____

    A. can readily be modified either in whole or in part
    B. must be made meaningful in some fashion to foster skills development
    C. can provide the sole source of group dynamics
    D. is one of the forces exerting influence on group members

18. According to the above passage, the members of the group   18.____

    A. should control their formation and development
    B. should control the circumstances of their meeting
    C. are influenced by the forces creating the group
    D. dissipate meaningless energy

19. According to the above passage, the effective group leader   19.____

    A. controls the focus of the group
    B. focuses his control over the group
    C. controls group forces by focusing upon group members
    D. focuses the group's forces upon himself

20. According to the above passage, effective leadership consists in

    A. partially compromising decision-making responsibilities
    B. partially sacrificing some basic responsibilities
    C. sometimes cultivating permissive subordinates
    D. providing participation for members of the group consistent with decision-making imperatives

20.____

Questions 21-22.

DIRECTIONS: Questions 21 and 22 are to be answered SOLELY on the basis of the following passage.

This country was built on the puritanical belief that honest toil was the foundation of moral rectitude, the cement of society, and the uphill road to progress. Idleness was sin. As a result, we treat free time today as a conditional joy. We permit outselves to relax only as a reward for hard work or as the recreation needed to put us back into shape for the job. Thus, the aimless delightful play of children gives way in adult life to a serious dedication to golf, the game that is so good for business.

21. According to the above passage, during former times in this country respectable work was considered to be MOST NEARLY a

    A. way to improve health
    B. form of recreation
    C. developer of good character
    D. reward for leisure

21.____

22. According to the point of view presented in the above passage, it would be MOST reasonable to assume that an employer would consider an employee's vacation to be a time for the employee to

    A. determine his own leisure time priorities
    B. loaf and relax
    C. learn new recreational skills
    D. increase his effectiveness at work

22.____

Questions 23-24.

DIRECTIONS: Questions 23 and 24 are to be answered SOLELY on the basis of the following passage.

A recent study revealed some very concrete evidence concerning the relationship between avocations and mental health. A number of well-adjusted persons were surveyed as to the type, number, and duration of their hobbies. The findings were compared to those from a similar survey of mentally disturbed persons. In the well-adjusted group, both the number of hobbies and the intensity with which they were pursued were far greater than that of the mentally disturbed group.

23. According to the above passage, the study showed that   23.____

    A. well-adjusted people engage in hobbies more widely and deeply than do mentally disturbed people
    B. hobbies, if taken seriously, serve to keep most people mentally well
    C. mental patients should be taught hobbies as a part of their therapy
    D. the degree of interest in hobbies plays an important role in maintaining good mental health

24. In reference to the study mentioned in the above passage, it is MOST accurate to say   24.____
that it appears to have

    A. been based on a carefully-structured, complex research design
    B. considered the variables of mental health and hobby involvement
    C. contained a general definition of mental health
    D. given evidence of a causal relationship between hobbies and mental health

25. Across the years, our social sense has decreed that every position of social leadership,   25.____
every place of influence, every concentration of social power in the hands of an individual, every instrument or agency that has aggregated to itself the power to affect the common welfare, has become by that very fact a social trust that must be administered for the common good. In our moral world, the social obligations of power are real and unescapable. On the basis of this statement, it would be MOST correct to state that

    A. an individual engaged in private enterprise does not have the social responsibility of one who holds public office
    B. social leadership carries with it the obligation to administer for the public good
    C. in our moral world, the abuse of the power is real and unescapable
    D. social leadership depends upon the aggregation of power in the hands of an individual or in an agency that wields concentrated influence

KEY (CORRECT ANSWERS)

1.	B		11.	D
2.	C		12.	C
3.	A		13.	A
4.	C		14.	A
5.	C		15.	C
6.	A		16.	C
7.	A		17.	D
8.	A		18.	C
9.	C		19.	C
10.	C		20.	D

21.	C
22.	D
23.	A
24.	B
25.	B

———

TEST 2

DIRECTIONS: Each question or incomplete statement is followed by several suggested answers or completions. Select the one that BEST answers the question or completes the statement. *PRINT THE LETTER OF THE CORRECT ANSWER IN THE SPACE AT THE RIGHT.*

Questions 1-9.

DIRECTIONS: Questions 1 through 9 are to be answered SOLELY on the basis of the following passage.

The establishment of a procedure whereby the client's rent is paid directly by the Social Service agency has been suggested recently by many people in the Social Service field. It is believed that such a procedure would be advantageous to both the agency and the client. Under the current system, clients often complain that their rent allowances are not for the correct amount. Agencies, in turn, have had to cope with irate landlords who complain that they are not receiving rent checks until much later than their due date.

The proposed new system would involve direct payment of the client's rent by the agency to the landlord. Clients would not receive a monthly rent allowance. Under one possible implementation of such a system, special rent payment offices would be set up in each borough and staffed by Social Service clerical personnel. Each office would handle all work involved in sending out monthly rent payments. Each client would receive monthly notification from the Social Service agency that his rent has been paid. A rent office would be established for every three Social Service centers in each borough. Only in cases where the rental exceeds $350 per month would payment be made and records kept by the Social Service center itself rather than a special rent office. However, clients would continue to make all direct contacts through the Social Service center.

Files in the rent offices would be organized on the basis of client rental. All cases involving monthly rents up to, but not exceeding, $300 would be placed in salmon-colored folders. Cases with rents from $300 to $500 would be placed in buff folders, and those with rents exceeding $500, but less than $750 would be filed in blue folders. If a client's rental changed, he would be required to notify the center as soon as possible so that this information could be brought up-to-date in his folder and the color of his folder changed if necessary. Included in the information needed, in addition to the amount of rent, are the size of the apartment, the type of heat, and the number of flights of stairs to climb if there is no elevator.

Discussion as to whether the same information should be required of clients residing in city projects was resolved with the decision that the identical system of filing and updating of files should apply to such project tenants. The basic problem that might arise from the institution of such a program is that clients would resent being unable to pay their own rent. However, it is likely that such resentment would be only a temporary reaction to change and would disappear after the new system became standard procedure. It has been suggested that this program first be experimented with on a small scale to determine what problems may arise and how the program can be best implemented.

1. According to the above passage, there a number of complaints about the current system of rent payments. Which of the following is a complaint expressed in the passage?

1.____

A. Landlords complain that clients sometimes pay the wrong amount for their rent.
B. Landlords complain that clients sometimes do not pay their rent on time.
C. Clients say that the Social Service agency sometimes does not mail the rent out on time.
D. Landlords say that they sometimes fail to receive a check for the rent.

2. Assume that there are 15 Social Service centers in Manhattan.
   According to the above passage, the number of rent offices that should be established in that borough under the new system is

   A. 1   B. 3   C. 5   D. 15

   2._____

3. According to the above passage, a client under the new system would receive

   A. a rent receipt from the landlord indicating that Social Services has paid the rent
   B. nothing since his rent has been paid by Social Services
   C. verification from the landlord that the rent was paid
   D. notices of rent payment from the Social Service agency

   3._____

4. According to the above passage, a case record involving a client whose rent has changed from $310 to $540 per month should be changed from a _____ folder to a _____ folder.

   A. blue; salmon-colored   B. buff; blue
   C. salmon-colored; blue   D. yellow; buff

   4._____

5. According to the above passage, if a client's rental is lowered because of violations in his building, he would be required to notify the

   A. building department   B. landlord
   C. rent payment office   D. Social Service center

   5._____

6. Which one of the following kinds of information about a rented apartment is NOT mentioned in the above passage as being necessary to include in the client's folder?
   The

   A. floor number, if in an apartment house with an elevator
   B. rental, if in a city project apartment
   C. size of the apartment, if in a two-family house
   D. type of heat, if in a city project apartment

   6._____

7. Assume that the rent payment proposal discussed in the above passage is approved and ready for implementation in the city.
   Which of the following actions is MOST in accordance with the proposal described in the above passage?

   A. Change over completely and quickly to the new system to avoid the confusion of having clients under both systems.
   B. Establish rent payment offices in all of the existing Social Service centers.
   C. Establish one small rent payment office in Manhattan for about six months.
   D. Set up an office in each borough and discontinue issuing rent allowances.

   7._____

8. According to the above passage, it can be inferred that the MOST important drawback of the new system would be that once a program is started clients might feel

   8._____

A. they have less independence than they had before
B. unable to cope with problems that mature people should be able to handle
C. too far removed from Social Service personnel to successfully adapt to the new requirements
D. too independent to work with the system

9. The above passage suggests that the proposed rent program be started as a pilot program rather than be instituted immediately throughout the city.   9.____
Of the following possible reasons for a pilot program, the one which is stated in the above passage as the MOST direct reason is that

A. any change made would then be only on a temporary basis
B. difficulties should be determined from small-scale implementation
C. implementation on a wide scale is extremely difficult
D. many clients might resent the new system

Questions 10-14.

DIRECTIONS: Questions 10 through 14 are to be answered SOLELY on the basis of the following passage.

PROCEDURE TO OBTAIN REIMBURSEMENT FROM DEPARTMENT OF HEALTH FOR CARE OF PHYSICALLY HANDICAPPED CHILDREN

Application for reimbursement must be received by the Department of Health within 30 days of the date of hospital admission in order that the Department of Hospitals may be reimbursed from the date of admission. Upon determination that patient is physically handicapped, as defined under Chapter 780 of the State Laws, the ward clerk shall prepare seven copies of Department of Health Form A-1 or A-2, Application and Authorization, and shall submit six copies to the institutional Collections Unit. The ward clerk shall also initiate two copies of Department of Health Form B-1 or B-2, Financial and Social Report, and shall forward them to the institutional Collections Unit for completion of Page 1 and routing to the Social Service Division for completion of the Social Summary on Page 2. Social Service Division shall return Form B-1 or B-2 to the institutional Collections Unit which shall forward one copy of Form B-1 or B-2 and six copies of Form A-1 or A-2 to Central Office Division of Collections for transmission to Bureau of Handicapped Children, Department of Health.

10. According to the above paragraph, the Department of Health will pay for hospital care for   10.____

A. children who are physically handicapped
B. any children who are ward patients
C. physically handicapped adults and children
D. thirty days for eligible children

11. According to the procedure described in the above paragraph, the definition of what constitutes a physical handicap is made by the   11.____

A. attending physician
B. laws of the State
C. Social Service Division
D. ward clerk

12. According to the above paragraph, Form B-1 or B-2 is   12.____

    A. a three page form containing detachable pages
    B. an authorization form issued by the Department of Hospitals
    C. completed by the ward clerk after the Social Summary has been entered
    D. sent to the institutional Collections Unit by the Social Service Division

13. According to the above paragraph, after their return by the Social Service Division, the   13.____
institutional Collections Unit keeps

    A. one copy of Form A-1 or A-2
    B. one copy of Form A-1 or A-2 and one copy of Form B-1 or B-2
    C. one copy of Form B-1 or B-2
    D. no copies of Forms A-1 or A-2 or B-1 or B-2

14. According to the above paragraph, forwarding the *Application and Authorization* to the   14.____
Department of Health is the responsibility of the

    A. Bureau for Handicapped Children
    B. Central Office Division of Collections
    C. Institutional Collections Unit
    D. Social Service Division

Questions 15-19.

DIRECTIONS: Questions 15 through 19 are to be answered SOLELY on the basis of the following *total annual income adjustment* rules for household income.

The basic annual income is to be calculated by multiplying the total of the current weekly salaries of all adults (age 21 or over) by 52.

Upward and downward adjustments must be made to the basic annual salary to arrive at the *total adjusted annual income* for the household.

UPWARD ADJUSTMENTS

1. Add one-half of total overtime payments in the previous two years.
2. Add that part of the earnings of any minor in the household that exceeded $3,000 in the previous 12 months.

DOWNWARD ADJUSTMENTS

1. Deduct one-third of all educational tuition payments for household members in the previous 12 months.
2. Deduct the expense of going to and from work in excess of $30 per week per household member. This adjustment is made on the basis of the previous 12 months and should be computed for each household member individually for each week in which excess travel expenses were incurred.
3. Deduct that part of child care expenses which exceeded $1,500 in the previous 12 months.

15. In Household A, the husband has a weekly salary of $585 and the wife has just had her   15._____
salary increased from $390 to $420 per week. In the previous 12 months, each had a
paid continuous vacation of four weeks; the husband had to travel to a secondary work
location every fourth week. His travel costs during those weeks were $42 per week.
In the previous 12 months, they had child care costs of $1,470.
What is the TOTAL annual adjusted income for the household?

    A. $52,116   B. $52,104   C. $51,828   D. $51,234

16. In Household B, the husband has a weekly salary of $540. In the past year, he received   16._____
overtime payments of $255. In the year before that, he received overtime payments of
$1,221. His wife has just begun a job with a weekly salary of $330. As a result of this,
annual child care expenses will be $2,130.
What is the TOTAL annual adjusted income for the household?

    A. $45,240   B. $45,348   C. $45,978   D. $46,824

17. In Household C, the husband has a weekly salary of $555. The wife has a weekly salary   17._____
of $390. They each had expenses of $33 per week when traveling to and from work in
the previous 12 months. The husband had an annual paid vacation of five weeks, and the
wife had an annual paid vacation of three weeks in the previous year. There is a daughter
in college for whom annual tuition payments of $1,710 were made in the previous 12
months.
What is the TOTAL annual adjusted income for the household?

    A. $48,258   B. $48,282   C. $49,140   D. $50,022

18. In Household D, the husband has a weekly salary of $465, the wife has a weekly salary   18._____
of $330, and an adult daughter has a weekly salary of $285. The husband received overtime payments of $1,890 in the past year. In the year before that, he received no over-
time payments. In the past year, there were weekly child care expenses of $210 per
week for 47 weeks.
What is the TOTAL adjusted annual income for the household?

    A. $57,105   B. $48,735   C. $47,235   D. $46,845

19. In Household E, the husband has a weekly salary of $615. The wife has a weekly salary   19._____
of $195. During the past year, there were tuition payments of $255 per month for 10
months per year for children in grade school and annual tuition payments of $2,310 for a
boy in high school. What is the TOTAL adjusted annual income for the household?

    A. $39,570   B. $39,690   C. $40,500   D. $42,120

Questions 20-22.

DIRECTIONS: Questions 20 through 22 are to be answered SOLELY on the basis of the following paragraph.

Effective December 1, 2004, tenants thereafter admitted to public housing projects shall
pay rents in accordance with Schedule DV if they are veterans of the Gulf War, and in
accordance with Schedule D if they are not Gulf War veterans. However, all recipients of
public assistance shall pay rents in accordance with Schedule DW. Tenants of public housing
projects prior to the effective date of this change will continue to pay rent in accordance with
Schedule C2 if they are veterans of the Iraqi War or the Gulf War, in accordance with

Schedule C if they are not such veterans, and in accordance with Schedule CW if they receive public assistance and if they are not eligible to use the C2 Schedule. In addition, effective December 1, 2004, when a tenant is accepted for assistance by the Department of Welfare, if such acceptance requires that the tenant pay a new rental as outlined above, the effective date of the new rental is to be the first of the month following the date that the tenant is accepted for assistance by the Department of Welfare instead of the first of the month following the date of application for public assistance.

20. John Jones, a Gulf War veteran, has been living in a public housing project since June 2003. He applied for public assistance on November 15, 2004 and was accepted for public assistance on December 17, 2004.
If he continues to receive public assistance, his present rent should be based on the _____ Schedule.

    A. C2   B. CW   C. DV   D. DW

20._____

21. Jack Smith, who is not a veteran, moves into a public housing project in January 2006. If it should become necessary for him to apply for public assistance on February 10, 2006 and should he be accepted for such assistance on March 5, 2006, the rent that he pays in March 2006 should be based on the _____ Schedule.

    A. C   B. CW   C. D   D. DW

21._____

22. John Doe, a veteran of the Iraqi War, was admitted to a public housing project in August 2004. He applied for public assistance on February 1, 2005 and was accepted for such assistance on March 1, 2005.
On April 1, 2005, his rent should

    A. change to the C2 Schedule
    B. remain on the C2 Schedule, as previously
    C. change to the CW Schedule
    D. remain on the CW Schedule, as previously

22._____

Questions 23-25.

DIRECTIONS: Questions 23 through 25 are to be answered SOLELY on the basis of the following paragraph.

It has been proposed that an act be passed to provide for family allowances in the form of cash payments, normally to mothers, for children under sixteen years of age. Allowances are supposed to be spent exclusively for the care and education of the children; otherwise, they may be discontinued. They would vary in amount according to the age of the child and would be conditional upon satisfactory school attendance and accomplishment. The allowance would be paid to all families, regardless of means, but income tax exemptions for dependents would be reduced in consequence. The act would also permit the withdrawal of children from school and their entrance into the labor market after completing eighth grade. However, there would be no financial advantage in sending a child to work since the allowances would approximate the child's net earnings. Proponents of this proposal claim as advantages that it would provide social justice by taking into account elements of family need not possible under any normal wage structure system, be simple to administer, encourage an increase in the birth rate, remove unwilling or incapable students from our middle schools, and provide financial aid to poor, large families without the stigma of public welfare.

23. According to the proposal, the one of the following factors which would be LEAST likely   23._____
to cause a variation in the amount of the allowance to a family or cause a discontinuance
of it is

   A. a change in family wealth
   B. poor school attendance record of a child
   C. a child's being left back
   D. use of the allowance money on a hobby of one of the parents

24. The LEAST accurate of the following statements concerning schooling under this pro-   24._____
posal is:

   A. A 14-year-old girl attending the 6th grade of elementary school will not be permitted to leave school, even though her school work is unsatisfactory.
   B. A poor family will be encouraged to continue the schooling of their 15-year-old
twins who are in the junior year of high school.
   C. A 14-year-old boy who has been graduated from elementary school, but whose
school attendance has been unsatisfactory, will not be permitted to attend high
school.
   D. The family of a 17-year-old high school senior who is an honor student will not
receive an allowance.

25. College attendance of bright children of poor families may be aided by this proposal   25._____
because

   A. such children will be assured of higher marks
   B. families are likely to be smaller and consequently parents will be better able to
send their children to college
   C. more scholarships are likely to be offered by private colleges as a result of this proposal
   D. the financial subsidy granted for a child under 16 may help the family save money
towards a college education

KEY (CORRECT ANSWERS)

1.	B	11.	B
2.	C	12.	D
3.	D	13.	C
4.	B	14.	B
5.	D	15.	A
6.	A	16.	C
7.	C	17.	B
8.	A	18.	B
9.	B	19.	C
10.	A	20.	A

21.	C
22.	B
23.	A
24.	C
25.	D

PREPARING WRITTEN MATERIAL

PARAGRAPH REARRANGEMENT
COMMENTARY

The sentences which follow are in scrambled order. You are to rearrange them in proper order and indicate the letter choice containing the correct answer at the space at the right.

Each group of sentences in this section is actually a paragraph presented in scrambled order. Each sentence in the group has a place in that paragraph; no sentence is to be left out. You are to read each group of sentences and decide upon the best order in which to put the sentences so as to form as well-organized paragraph.

The questions in this section measure the ability to solve a problem when all the facts relevant to its solution are not given.

More specifically, certain positions of responsibility and authority require the employee to discover connections between events sometimes, apparently, unrelated. In order to do this, the employee will find it necessary to correctly infer that unspecified events have probably occurred or are likely to occur. This ability becomes especially important when action must be taken on incomplete information.

Accordingly, these questions require competitors to choose among several suggested alternatives, each of which presents a different sequential arrangement of the events. Competitors must choose the MOST logical of the suggested sequences.

In order to do so, they may be required to draw on general knowledge to infer missing concepts or events that are essential to sequencing the given events. Competitors should be careful to infer only what is essential to the sequence. The plausibility of the wrong alternatives will always require the inclusion of unlikely events or of additional chains of events which are NOT essential to sequencing the given events.

It's very important to remember that you are looking for the best of the four possible choices, and that the best choice of all may not even be one of the answers you're given to choose from.

There is no one right way to these problems. Many people have found it helpful to first write out the order of the sentences, as they would have arranged them, on their scrap paper before looking at the possible answers. If their optimum answer is there, this can save them some time. If it isn't, this method can still give insight into solving the problem. Others find it most helpful to just go through each of the possible choices, contrasting each as they go along. You should use whatever method feels comfortable, and works, for you.

While most of these types of questions are not that difficult, we've added a higher percentage of the difficult type, just to give you more practice. Usually there are only one or two questions on this section that contain such subtle distinctions that you're unable to answer confidently, and you then may find yourself stuck deciding between two possible choices, neither of which you're sure about.

———

EXAMINATION SECTION
TEST 1

DIRECTIONS: The sentences that follow are in scrambled order. You are to rearrange them in proper order and indicate the letter choice containing the correct answer. *PRINT THE LETTER OF THE CORRECT ANSWER IN THE SPACE AT THE RIGHT.*

1. Below are four statements labeled W., X., Y., and Z. 1.____
   W. He was a strict and fanatic drillmaster.
   X. The word is always used in a derogatory sense and generally shows resentment and anger on the part of the user.
   Y. It is from the name of this Frenchman that we derive our English word, martinet.
   Z. Jean Martinet was the Inspector-General of Infantry during the reign of King Louis XIV.
   The *PROPER* order in which these sentences should be placed in a paragraph is:

   A. X, Z, W, Y   B. X, Z, Y, W   C. Z, W, Y, X   D. Z, Y, W, X

2. In the following paragraph, the sentences which are numbered, have been jumbled. 2.____
   1. Since then it has undergone changes.
   2. It was incorporated in 1955 under the laws of the State of New York.
   3. Its primary purpose, a cleaner city, has, however, remained the same.
   4. The Citizens Committee works in cooperation with the Mayor's Inter-departmental Committee for a Clean City.
   The order in which these sentences should be arranged to form a well-organized paragraph is:

   A. 2, 4, 1, 3   B. 3, 4, 1, 2   C. 4, 2, 1, 3   D. 4, 3, 2, 1

Questions 3-5.

DIRECTIONS: The sentences listed below are part of a meaningful paragraph but they are not given in their proper order. You are to decide what would be the *best order* in which to put the sentences so as to form a well-organized paragraph. Each sentence has a place in the paragraph; there are no extra sentences. You are then to answer questions 3 to 5 inclusive on the basis of your rearrangements of these secrambled sentences into a properly organized paragraph.

In 1887 some insurance companies organized an Inspection Department to advise their clients on all phases of fire prevention and protection. Probably this has been due to the smaller annual fire losses in Great Britain than in the United States. It tests various fire prevention devices and appliances and determines manufacturing hazards and their safeguards. Fire research began earlier in the United States and is more advanced than in Great Britain. Later they established a laboratory specializing in electrical, mechanical, hydraulic, and chemical fields.

3. When the five sentences are arranged in proper order, the paragraph starts with the sentence which begins   3._____

    A. "In 1887..."   B. "Probably this ..."   C. "It tests ..."
    D. "Fire research ..."   E. "Later they ..."

4. In the last sentence listed above, "they" refers to   4._____

    A. insurance companies
    B. the United States and Great Britain
    C. the Inspection Department
    D. clients
    E. technicians

5. When the above paragraph is properly arranged, it ends with the words   5._____

    A. "... and protection."   B. "... the United States."
    C. "... their safeguards."   D. "... in Great Britain."
    E. "... chemical fields."

———

KEY (CORRECT ANSWERS)

    1. C
    2. C
    3. D
    4. A
    5. C

———

TEST 2

1. 1. It is established when one shows that the landlord has prevented the tenant's enjoyment of his interest in the property leased.
    2. Constructive eviction is the result of a breach of the covenant of quiet enjoyment implied in all leases.
    3. In some parts of the United States, it is not complete until the tenant vacates within a reasonable time.
    4. Generally, the acts must be of such serious and permanent character as to deny the tenant the enjoyment of his possessing rights.
    5. In this event, upon abandonment of the premises, the tenant's liability for that ceases.

    The CORRECT answer is:

    A. 2, 1, 4, 3, 5   B. 5, 2, 3, 1, 4   C. 4, 3, 1, 2, 5
    D. 1, 3, 5, 4, 2

    1.____

2. 1. The powerlessness before private and public authorities that is the typical experience of the slum tenant is reminiscent of the situation of blue-collar workers all through the nineteenth century.
    2. Similarly, in recent years, this chapter of history has been reopened by anti-poverty groups which have attempted to organize slum tenants to enable them to bargain collectively with their landlords about the conditions of their tenancies.
    3. It is familiar history that many of the workers remedied their condition by joining together and presenting their demands collectively.
    4. Like the workers, tenants are forced by the conditions of modern life into substantial dependence on these who possess great political arid economic power.
    5. What's more, the very fact of dependence coupled with an absence of education and self-confidence makes them hesitant and unable to stand up for what they need from those in power.

    The CORRECT answer is:

    A. 5, 4, 1, 2, 3   B. 2, 3, 1, 5, 4   C. 3, 1, 5, 4, 2
    D. 1, 4, 5, 3, 2

    2.____

3. 1. A railroad, for example, when not acting as a common carrier may contract; away responsibility for its own negligence.
    2. As to a landlord, however, no decision has been found relating to the legal effect of a clause shifting the statutory duty of repair to the tenant.
    3. The courts have not passed on the validity of clauses relieving the landlord of this duty and liability.
    4. They have, however, upheld the validity of exculpatory clauses in other types of contracts.
    5. Housing regulations impose a duty upon the landlord to maintain leased premises in safe condition.

    3.____

6. As another example, a bailee may limit his liability except for gross negligence, willful acts, or fraud.

The CORRECT answer is:

A. 2, 1, 6, 4, 3, 5   B. 1, 3, 4, 5, 6, 2   C. 3, 5, 1, 4, 2, 6
D. 5, 3, 4, 1, 6, 2

4. 1. Since there are only samples in the building, retail or consumer sales are generally 4.____
eschewed by mart occupants, and,in some instances, rigid controls are maintained
to limit entrance to the mart only to those persons engaged in retailing.
 2. Since World War I, in many larger cities, there has developed a new type of
property, called the mart building.
 3. It can, therefore, be used by wholesalers and jobbers for the display of sample
merchandise.
 4. This type of building is most frequently a multi-storied, finished interior property
which is a cross between a retail arcade and a loft building.
 5. This limitation enables the mart occupants to ship the orders from another location after the retailer or dealer makes his selection from the samples.

The CORRECT answer is:

A. 2, 4, 3, 1, 5   B. 4, 3, 5, 1, 2   C. 1, 3, 2, 4, 5
D. 1, 4, 2, 3, 5

5. 1. In general, staff-line friction reduces the distinctive contribution of staff personnel. 5.____
 2. The conflicts, however, introduce an uncontrolled element into the managerial
system.
 3. On the other hand, the natural resistance of the line to staff innovations probably
usefully restrains over-eager efforts to apply untested procedures on a large
scale.
 4. Under such conditions, it is difficult to know when valuable ideas are being sacri-
ficed.
 5. The relatively weak position of staff, requiring accommodation to the line, tends
to restrict their ability to engage .in free, experimental innovation.

The CORRECT answer is:

A. 4, 2, 3, 1, 3   B. 1, 5, 3, 2, 4   C. 5, 3, 1, 2, 4
D. 2, 1, 4, 5, 3

KEY (CORRECT ANSWERS)

1. A
2. D
3. D
4. A
5. B

TEST 3

DIRECTIONS: Questions 1 through 4 consist of six sentences which can be arranged in a logical sequence. For each question, select the choice which places the numbered sentences in the *most logical* sequence. *PRINT THE LETTER OF THE CORRECT ANSWER IN THE SPACE AT THE RIGHT.*

1. 1. The burden of proof as to each issue is determined before trial and remains upon the same party throughout the trial.
    2. The jury is at liberty to believe one witness' testimony as against a number of contradictory witnesses.
    3. In a civil case, the party bearing the burden of proof is required to prove his contention by a fair preponderance of the evidence.
    4. However, it must be noted that a fair preponderance of evidence does not necessarily mean a greater number of witnesses.
    5. The burden of proof is the burden which rests upon one of the parties to an action to persuade the trier of the facts, generally the jury, that a proposition he asserts is true.
    6. If the evidence is equally balanced, or if it leaves the jury in such doubt as to be unable to decide the controversy either way, judgment must be given against the party upon whom the burden of proof rests.

    The CORRECT answer is:

    A. 3, 2, 5, 4, 1, 6   B. 1, 2, 6, 5, 3, 4   C. 3, 4, 5, 1, 2, 6
    D. 5, 1, 3, 6, 4, 2

1.____

2. 1. If a parent is without assets and is unemployed, he cannot be convicted of the crime of non-support of a child.
    2. The term "sufficient ability" has been held to mean sufficient financial ability.
    3. It does not matter if his unemployment is by choice or unavoidable circumstances.
    4. If he fails to take any steps at all, he may be liable to prosecution for endangering the welfare of a child.
    5. Under the penal law, a parent is responsible for the support of his minor child only if the parent is "of sufficient ability."
    6. An indigent parent may meet his obligation by borrowing money or by seeking aid under the provisions of the Social Welfare Law.

    The CORRECT answer is:

    A. 6, 1, 5, 3, 2, 4   B. 1, 3, 5, 2, 4, 6   C. 5, 2, 1, 3, 6, 4
    D. 1, 6, 4, 5, 2, 3

2.____

3. 1. Consider, for example, the case of a rabble rouser who urges a group of twenty people to go out and break the windows of a nearby factory.
    2. Therefore, the law fills the indicated gap with the crime of inciting to riot."
    3. A person is considered guilty of inciting to riot when he urges ten or more persons to engage in tumultuous and violent conduct of a kind likely to create public alarm.
    4. However, if he has not obtained the cooperation of at least four people, he cannot be charged with unlawful assembly.
    5. The charge of inciting to riot was added to the law to cover types of conduct which cannot be classified as either the crime of "riot" or the crime of "unlawful assembly."
    6. If he acquires the acquiescence of at least four of them, he is guilty of unlawful assembly even if the project does not materialize.

The CORRECT answer is:

A. 3, 5, 1, 6, 4, 2   B. 5, 1, 4, 6, 2, 3   C. 3, 4, 1, 5, 2, 6
D. 5, 1, 4, 6, 3, 2

3.____

4. 1. If, however, the rebuttal evidence presents an issue of credibility, it is for the jury to determine whether the presumption has, in fact, been destroyed.
    2. Once sufficient evidence to the contrary is introduced, the presumption disappears from the trial.
    3. The effect of a presumption is to place the burden upon the adversary to come forward with evidence to rebut the presumption.
    4. When a presumption is overcome and ceases to exist in the case, the fact or facts which gave rise to the presumption still remain.
    5. Whether a presumption has been overcome is ordinarily a question for the court.
    6. Such information may furnish a basis for a logical inference.

The CORRECT answer is:

A. 4, 6, 2, 5, 1, 3   B. 3, 2, 5, 1, 4, 6   C. 5, 3, 6, 4, 2, 1
D. 5, 4, 1, 2, 6, 3

4.____

KEY (CORRECT ANSWERS)

1. D
2. C
3. A
4. B

PREPARING WRITTEN MATERIAL

EXAMINATION SECTION
TEST 1

DIRECTIONS: Each question consists of a sentence which may or may not be an example of good English usage. Examine each sentence, considering grammar, punctuation, spelling, capitalization, and awkwardness. Then choose the correct statement about it from the four choices below it. If the English usage in the sentence given is better than any of the changes suggested in choices B, C, or D, pick choice A. (Do not pick a choice that will change the meaning of the sentence.)

1. We attended a staff conference on Wednesday the new safety and fire rules were discussed.

    A. This is an example of acceptable writing.
    B. The words "safety," "fire" and "rules" should begin with capital letters.
    C. There should be a comma after the word "Wednesday."
    D. There should be a period after the word "Wednesday" and the word "the" should begin with a capital letter

1.____

2. Neither the dictionary or the telephone directory could be found in the office library.

    A. This is an example of acceptable writing.
    B. The word "or" should be changed to "nor."
    C. The word "library" should be spelled "libery."
    D. The word "neither" should be changed to "either."

2.____

3. The report would have been typed correctly if the typist could read the draft.

    A. This is an example of acceptable writing.
    B. The word "would" should be removed.
    C. The word "have" should be inserted after the word "could."
    D. The word "correctly" should be changed to "correct."

3.____

4. The supervisor brought the reports and forms to an employees desk.

    A. This is an example of acceptable writing.
    B. The word "brought" should be changed to "took."
    C. There should be a comma after the word "reports" and a comma after the word "forms."
    D. The word "employees" should be spelled "employee's."

4.____

5. It's important for all the office personnel to submit their vacation schedules on time.

    A. This is an example of acceptable writing.
    B. The word "It's" should be spelled "Its."
    C. The word "their" should be spelled "they're."
    D. The word "personnel" should be spelled "personal."

5.____

6. The report, along with the accompanying documents, were submitted for review.   6.____

   A. This is an example of acceptable writing.
   B. The words "were submitted" should be changed to "was submitted."
   C. The word "accompanying" should be spelled "accompaning."
   D. The comma after the word "report" should be taken out.

7. If others must use your files, be certain that they understand how the system works, but   7.____
   insist that you do all the filing and refiling.

   A. This is an example of acceptable writing.
   B. There should be a period after the word "works," and the word "but" should start a
      new sentence
   C. The words "filing" and "refiling" should be spelled "fileing" and "refileing."
   D. There should be a comma after the word "but."

8. The appeal was not considered because of its late arrival.   8.____

   A. This is an example of acceptable writing.
   B. The word "its" should be changed to "it's."
   C. The word "its" should be changed to "the."
   D. The words "late arrival" should be changed to "arrival late."

9. The letter must be read carefuly to determine under which subject it should be filed.   9.____

   A. This is an example of acceptable writing.
   B. The word "under" should be changed to "at."
   C. The word "determine" should be spelled "determin."
   D. The word "carefuly" should be spelled "carefully."

10. He showed potential as an office manager, but he lacked skill in delegating work.   10.____

   A. This is an example of acceptable writing.
   B. The word "delegating" should be spelled "delagating."
   C. The word "potential" should be spelled "potencial."
   D. The words "he lacked" should be changed to "was lacking."

KEY (CORRECT ANSWERS)

1.	D	6.	B
2.	B	7.	A
3.	C	8.	A
4.	D	9.	D
5.	A	10.	A

TEST 2

DIRECTIONS: DIRECTIONS: Each question consists of a sentence which may or may not be an example of good English usage. Examine each sentence, considering grammar, punctuation, spelling, capitalization, and awkwardness. Then choose the correct statement about it from the four choices below it. If the English usage in the sentence given is better than any of the changes suggested in choices B, C, or D, pick choice A. (Do not pick a choice that will change the meaning of the sentence.)

1. The supervisor wants that all staff members report to the office at 9:00 A.M. 1.____

   A. This is an example of acceptable writing.
   B. The word "that" should be removed and the word "to" should be inserted after the word "members."
   C. There should be a comma after the word "wants" and a comma after the word "office."
   D. The word "wants" should be changed to "want" and the word "shall" should be inserted after the word "members."

2. Every morning the clerk opens the office mail and distributes it . 2.____

   A. This is an example of acceptable writing.
   B. The word "opens" should be changed to "open."
   C. The word "mail" should be changed to "letters."
   D. The word "it" should be changed to "them."

3. The secretary typed more fast on a desktop computer than on a laptop computer. 3.____

   A. This is an example of acceptable writing.
   B. The words "more fast" should be changed to "faster."
   C. There should be a comma after the words "desktop computer."
   D. The word "than" should be changed to "then."

4. The new stenographer needed a desk a computer, a chair and a blotter. 4.____

   A. This is an example of acceptable writing.
   B. The word "blotter" should be spelled "blodder."
   C. The word "stenographer" should begin with a capital letter.
   D. There should be a comma after the word "desk."

5. The recruiting officer said, "There are many different goverment jobs available." 5.____

   A. This is an example of acceptable writing.
   B. The word "There" should not be capitalized.
   C. The word "goverment" should be spelled "government".
   D. The comma after the word "said" should be removed.

6. He can recommend a mechanic whose work is reliable. 6.____

   A. This is an example of acceptable writing.
   B. The word "reliable" should be spelled "relyable."
   C. The word "whose" should be spelled "who's."
   D. The word "mechanic" should be spelled "mecanic."

7. She typed quickly; like someone who had not a moment to lose.   7.____

    A. This is an example of acceptable writing.
    B. The word "not" should be removed.
    C. The semicolon should be changed to a comma.
    D. The word "quickly" should be placed before instead of after the word "typed."

8. She insisted that she had to much work to do.   8.____

    A. This is an example of acceptable writing.
    B. The word "insisted" should be spelled "incisted."
    C. The word "to" used in front of "much" should be spelled "too."
    D. The word "do" should be changed to "be done."

9. He excepted praise from his supervisor for a job well done.   9.____

    A. This is an example of acceptable writing.
    B. The word "excepted" should be spelled "accepted."
    C. The order of the words "well done" should be changed to "done well."
    D. There should be a comma after the word "supervisor."

10. What appears to be intentional errors in grammar occur several times in the passage.   10.____

    A. This is an example of acceptable writing.
    B. The word "occur" should be spelled "occurr."
    C. The word "appears" should be changed to "appear."
    D. The phrase "several times" should be changed to "from time to time."

KEY (CORRECT ANSWERS)

1.	B		6.	A
2.	A		7.	C
3.	B		8.	C
4.	D		9.	B
5.	C		10.	C

TEST 3

Questions 1-5.

DIRECTIONS: Same as for Tests 1 and 2.

1. The clerk could have completed the assignment on time if he knows where these materi-   1.____
    als were located.

    A. This is an example of acceptable writing.
    B. The word "knows" should be replaced by "had known."
    C. The word "were" should be replaced by "had been."
    D. The words "where these materials were located" should be replaced by "the loca-
        tion of these materials."

2. All employees should be given safety training. Not just those who have accidents.   2.____

    A. This is an example of acceptable writing.
    B. The period after the word "training" should be changed to a colon.
    C. The period after the word "training" should be changed to a semicolon, and the first
        letter of the word "Not" should be changed to a small "n."
    D. The period after the word "training" should be changed to a comma, and the first
        letter of the word "Not" should be changed to a small "n."

3. This proposal is designed to promote employee awareness of the suggestion program, to   3.____
    encourage employee participation in the program, and to increase the number of
    suggestions submitted.

    A. This is an example of acceptable writing.
    B. The word "proposal" should be spelled "preposal."
    C. The words "to increase the number of suggestions submitted" should be changed
        to "an increase in the number of suggestions is expected."
    D. The word "promote" should be changed to "enhance" and the word "increase"
        should be changed to "add to."

4. The introduction of inovative managerial techniques should be preceded by careful anal-   4.____
    ysis of the specific circumstances and conditions in each department.

    A. This is an example of acceptable writing.
    B. The word "techniques" should be spelled "techneques."
    C. The word "inovative" should be spelled "innovative."
    D. A comma should be placed after the word "circumstances" and after the word "con-
        ditions."

5. This occurrence indicates that such criticism embarrasses him.   5.____

    A. This is an example of acceptable writing.
    B. The word "occurrence" should be spelled "occurence."
    C. The word "criticism" should be spelled "critisism."
    D. The word "embarrasses" should be spelled "embarasses."

————————

KEY (CORRECT ANSWERS)

1. B
2. D
3. A
4. C
5. A

———

ARITHMETICAL REASONING
EXAMINATION SECTION
TEST 1

DIRECTIONS: Each question or incomplete statement is followed by several suggested answers or completions. Select the one that BEST answers the question or completes the statement. *PRINT THE LETTER OF THE CORRECT ANSWER IN THE SPACE AT THE RIGHT.*

1. On January 1, a family was receiving supplementary monthly public assistance of $280   1.____
for food, $240 for rent, and $140 for other necessities. In the spring, their rent rose by
10%, and their rent allotment was adjusted accordingly. In the summer, due to the death
of a family member, their allotments for food and other necessities were reduced by 1/7.
Their monthly allowance check in the fall should be

   A. $624   B. $644   C. $664   D. $684

2. Twice a month, a certain family receives a $340 general allowance for rent, food, and   2.____
clothing expenses. In addition, the family receives a specific supplementary allotment for
utilities of $384 a year, which is added to their semi-monthly check.
If the general allowance alone is reduced by 5%, what will be the TOTAL amount of
their next semi-monthly check?

   A. $323   B. $339   C. $340   D. $355

3. If each supervising clerk in a certain unit sees an average of 9 clients in a 7-hour day and   3.____
there are 15 supervising clerks in the unit, APPROXIMATELY how many clients will be
seen in a 35-hour week?

   A.   315   B.   405   C.   675   D.   945

4. In one day, an aide receives 18 inquiries by phone and 27 inquiries in person.   4.____
What percentage of the inquiries received that day were by phone?

   A.   33%   B.   40%   C.   45%   D.   60%

5. If the weekly paychecks for 5 employees are $258.64, $325.48, $287.34, $271.50, and   5.____
$313.12, then the combined weekly income for the 5 employees is

   A. $1,455.68   B. $1,456.08   C. $1,461.68   D. $1,474.08

6. Suppose that there are 17 aides working in an office where many community complaints   6.____
are received by telephone. In one ten-day period, 4,250 calls were received.
If the same number of calls were received each day, and the aides divided the work
load equally, about how many calls did each aide respond to daily?

   A.   25   B.   35   C.   75   D.   250

7. Suppose that an assignment was divided among 5 aides. If the first aide spent 67 hours   7.____
on the assignment, the second aide spent 95 hours, the third aide spent 52 hours, the
fourth aide spent 78 hours, and the fifth aide spent 103 hours, what was the AVERAGE
amount of time spent by each aide on the assignment?
_____ hours.

   A.   71   B.   75   C.   79   D.   83

8. If there are 240 employees in a center and 1/3 are absent on the day of a bad snow-
   storm, how many employees were at work in the center on that day?

   A. 80   B. 120   C. 160   D. 200

   8.____

9. Suppose that an aide takes 25 minutes to prepare a letter to a client.
   If the aide is assigned to prepare 9 letters on a certain day, how much time should she
   set aside for this task? _____ hours.

   A. 3 3/4   B. 4 1/4   C. 4 3/4   D. 5 1/4

   9.____

10. Suppose that a certain center uses both Form A and Form B in the course of its daily
    work and that Form A is used 4 times as often as Form B.
    If the total number of both forms used in one week is 750, how many times was Form
    A used?

    A. 100   B. 200   C. 400   D. 600

    10.____

11. Suppose a center has a budget of $2,185.40 from which 8 desks costing $156.10 apiece
    must be bought.
    How many additional desks can be ordered from this budget after the 8 desks have
    been purchased?

    A. 4   B. 6   C. 9   D. 14

    11.____

12. When researching a particular case, a team of 16 aides was asked to check through 234
    folders to obtain the necessary information.
    If half the aides worked twice as fast as the other half, and the slow group checked
    through 12 folders each hour, about how long would it take to complete the assign-
    ment? _____ hours.

    A. 4 1/4   B. 5   C. 6   D. 6 1/2

    12.____

13. The difference in the cost of two typewriters is $56.64. If the less expensive typewriter
    costs $307.22, what is the cost of the other typewriter?

    A. $343.86   B. $344.06   C. $363.86   D. $364.06

    13.____

14. At the start of a year, a family was receiving a public assistance grant of $382 twice a
    month, on the 1st and 15th of each month. On March 1, their rent allowance was
    decreased from $150 to $142 a month since they had moved to a smaller apartment. On
    August 1, their semi-monthly food allowance, which had been $80.40, was raised by
    10%. In that year, the TOTAL amount of money disbursed to this family was

    A. $4,544.20   B. $6,581.40   C. $9,088.40   D. $9,168.40

    14.____

15. It is discovered that a client has received double public assistance for 2 months by hav-
    ing been enrolled at two service centers of the Department of Social Services.
    The client should have received $168 twice a month instead of the double amount. He
    now agrees to repay the money by equal deductions from his public assistance check
    over a period of 12 months. What will the amount of his NEXT check be?

    A. $112   B. $140   C. $154   D. $160

    15.____

16. Suppose a study is being made of the composition of 3,550 families receiving public assistance. Of the first 1,050 families reviewed, 18% had four or more children.
If, in the remaining number of families, the percentage with four or more children is half as high as the percentage in the group already reviewed, then the percentage of families with four or more children in the entire group of families is MOST NEARLY

    A. 12   B. 14   C. 16   D. 27

16._____

17. Suppose that food prices have risen 13%, and an increase of the same amount has been granted in the food allotment given to people receiving public assistance.
If a family has been receiving $810 a month, 35% of which is allotted for food, then the TOTAL amount of public assistance this family receives per month will be changed to

    A. $805.42   B. $840.06   C. $846.86   D. $899.42

17._____

18. Assume that the food allowance is to be raised 5% in August but will be retroactive for four months to April.
The retroactive allowance is to be divided into equal sections and added to the public assistance checks for August, September, October, November, and December. A family which has been receiving $840 monthly, 40% of which was allotted for food, will receive what size check in August?

    A. $853.44   B. $856.80   C. $861.00   D. $870.24

18._____

19. A blind client, who receives $210 public assistance twice a month, inherits 14 shares of stock worth $180 each.
The client is required to sell the stock and spend his inheritance before receiving more public assistance. Using his public assistance allowance as a guide, how many months are his new assets expected to last?

    A. 6   B. 7   C. 8   D. 12

19._____

20. The Department of Social Services has 16 service centers. These centers may be divided into those which are downtown and those which are uptown. Two of the centers are special service centers and are downtown, while the remainder of the centers are general service centers. There is a total of 7 service centers downtown.
The percentage of the general service centers which are uptown is MOST NEARLY

    A. 56   B. 64   C. 69   D. 79

20._____

21. For six months, a family lived in a 4-room apartment where they paid $380 a month. They made an intrasite move to a 4-room apartment where they paid $85 per room a month for six months.
Comparing the two six-month periods, the TOTAL amount of money the family saved by making the intrasite move was

    A. $240   B. $290   C. $430   D. $590

21._____

22. To calculate a tenant's usable income, you should make Social Security deductions of 4.4 percent on salary up to a maximum of $9,000 and State Disability deductions of .5 percent on salary up to $3,000.
What does a tenant's combined deduction amount to if his annual salary is $13,400?

    A. $411.00   B. $568.60   C. $619.60   D. $700.00

22._____

23. If the temporary relocation expenses for housing are set at $18 per day for one adult and $10 per day for each additional person in a room, how much money is allowed for a woman and four children temporarily relocated in one room for a period of six days?

   A. $168   B. $348   C. $378   D. $518

23._____

24. According to relocation policy, a family relocating to private housing from federally-aided or certain other sites will be granted a relocation payment. This payment equals the difference between 1/5 of the family's yearly income and the scheduled yearly rent for a standard apartment for their size family.
Suppose a 2-person family whose yearly income is $12,900 has been unable to obtain public housing and so finds a one-bedroom private apartment. The scheduled rent for a one-bedroom apartment appropriate for their occupancy is $240 a month. What payment will they receive?

   A. $240   B. $288   C. $300   D. $410

24._____

25. A family on a housing relocation site is paying $410 per month for rent. This represents 25% of their gross monthly income.
If the husband earns 4/5 of their total combined monthly income, how much does the wife earn per month?

   A. $328   B. $540   C. $1,280   D. $1,600

25._____

KEY (CORRECT ANSWERS)

1.	A		11.	B
2.	B		12.	D
3.	C		13.	C
4.	B		14.	D
5.	B		15.	B
6.	A		16.	A
7.	C		17.	C
8.	C		18.	D
9.	A		19.	A
10.	D		20.	B

21.	A
22.	A
23.	B
24.	C
25.	A

SOLUTIONS TO PROBLEMS

1. After spring, the rent allotment should be $(240+24) = $264 After the summer, the reduced allotment for food and other necessities should be $[(280+140)-1/7(280+140)] = $[(420 - 1/7(420)] = $(420-60) = $360. ∴ The monthly check in the fall including rent, food, and other necessities should be $360 + $264 = $624

2. Amount of general allowance in the family's semi-monthly check = $340. Amount of utilities allotment in the family's semi-monthly check: $$\$(\frac{384}{12} \times \frac{1}{2}) = \$16$$ Amount of general allowance in family's semi-monthly check after a 5% reduction = $340 less 5% of $340 = $(340-17) = $323 Total amount of the next month's semi-monthly check: Reduced general allowance + utilities allotment = $323 + $16 = $339

3. During 7 hours, a total of (15)(9) = 135 clients can be seen. Thus, in 35 hours, a total of (135)(5) = 675 clients will be seen.

4. 18/(18+27) = .40 = 40%

5. $258.64 + $325.48 + $287.34 + $271.50 + $313.12 = $1456.08

6. 4250 / 10 = 425 calls per day. Then, 425 / 17 = 25

7. (67+95+52+78+103) / 5 = 79 hours

8. Number present = (240)(2/3) = 160

9. (25)(9) = 225 min. = 3 hrs. 45 min. = 3 3/4 hrs.

10. Let x, 1/4x = number of forms A, B, respectively. Then, x + 1/4 x = 750. Solving, x = 600

11. $2185.40 - (8)($156.10) = $936.60. Then, $936.60 v 156.10 = 6 desks

12. Since the slow group did 12 folders each hour, the faster group did 24 folders each hour. Then, 234 / (12+24) = 6 1/2 hrs.

13. Expensive typewriter costs $307.22 + $56.64 = $363.86

14. For months of January and February, the amount the family receives is $(382x2x2) = $1528
For months of March through July, the family receives $(764-8) x 5 = $3780
For months of August through December, the family receives $(756+16.08) x 5 = $3860.40 The total amount of money disbursed to this family is $1528 + $3780 + $3860.40 = $9,168.40

15. The overpayment for 2 months = ($168)(4) = $672. If this is paid back over 12 months, each month's amount is reduced by $672 / 12 = $56. Then, each check (semi-monthly) is reduced by $28. His next check will be $168 - $28 = $140

16. (1050)(.18) + (2500)(.09) = 414. Then, 414 / 3550 = 12%

17. ($810)(.35) = $283.50 originally allotted for food. The new food allotment = ($283.50)(1.13) = $320.355. The total assistance now = $810 - $283.50 + $320.355 = $846.855 or $846.86

18. ($840)(.40) = $336 per month for food. The new food allowance = ($336)(1.05) = $352.80 per month. The difference of $16.80 is retroactive to April, which means ($16.80)(9) = $151.20 additional money for August through December. Each check for these 5 months will be increased by $15.20 / 5 = 30.24. Thus, the check in August = $840 + 30.24 = $870.24

19. ($180)(14) = $2520. Then, $2520 / $420 = 6 months

20. 5 general are -downtown; ... 9 of 14 general are uptown; 9 / 14 $\approx$ 64%.

21. ($85)(4) = $340 per month. Savings per month = $380 - $340 = $40 For six months, the savings = $240

22. ($9000)(.044) + ($3000)(.005) = $411 total deductions

23. ($18+$40)(6) = $348 relocation expenses

24. ($240)(12) - (1/5)($12,900) = $300 relocation payment

25. $410 $\div$ .25 = $1640. The wife earns (1640)(1/5) = $328 each month.

TEST 2

DIRECTIONS: Each question or incomplete statement is followed by several suggested answers or completions. Select the one that BEST answers the question or completes the statement. *PRINT THE LETTER OF THE CORRECT ANSWER IN THE SPACE AT THE RIGHT.*

1. A project tenant who owns and drives a taxicab for a living, reports for a three-month period, an income of $6,250 after operating expenses of $1,300 have been considered. In addition, his tips are valued at 12% of his income before operating expenses. An estimate of his yearly income is MOST NEARLY   1.____

    A. $22,000   B. $23,000   C. $28,000
    D. $28,500   E. $29,000

2. The maximum annual subsidy which can be paid by the State toward the operation of any low-rent housing project is the sum of the annual interest on the total original loan for building the project and 1% of the portion of the loan actually spent. If the original loan for a project was $8,000,000 at 1 3/4% interest, but only $7,500,000 was actually spent, then the MAXIMUM annual subsidy is   2.____

    A. $140,000   B. $145,000   C. $215,000
    D. $220,000   E. 271,250

3. In 2003, the cost of repairs and maintenance at a certain housing project was $5,589 · more than in 2002, representing an increase of 4.6%. A further increase at the same rate was anticipated for 2004. The cost of repairs and maintenance in 2004 was MOST NEARLY   3.____

    A. $127,100
    B. $132,700
    C. $132,900
    D. $133,000
    E. an amount which cannot be determined from the given data

4. Each day a delivery truck used by the Housing Authority travels 25 miles from a project to a storehouse and 25 miles on the return trip. It travels at the rate of 30 miles per hour going to the storehouse and at the rate of 20 miles per hour returning. The average rate, in miles per hour, for the roundtrip is MOST NEARLY   4.____

    A. 24
    B. 25
    C. 26
    D. the square root of 600
    E. an amount which cannot be determined from the given data 0

5. A report on the first 6,000 applications for apartments in a certain project containing 1,400 apartments indicated that those who were ineligible fell into four categories: 2,800 ineligible for reason A, 600 ineligible for reason B, 1,200 ineligible for reason C, and 400 ineligible for reason D. If the same proportions continue for the remaining 21,500 applications, then the percentage of eligible applicants who can be given apartments in the project is MOST NEARLY   5.____

    A. 25   B. 30   C. 33   D. 40   E. 60

6. The number of applications for apartments in low-rent housing projects was 40,000 in 1999. The number of applications increased 5% in 2000, and increased again in 2001 by 6% over the 2000 total.
The percentage by which the 2001 figures exceed the 1999 figures is

6.____

    A. 5.3   B. 6.0   C. 11.0   D. 11.3   E. 30.0

7. A rectangular lot, 75 feet by 11.0 feet, was purchased as part of a project site for $28,500.
The price per square foot of this lot is MOST NEARLY

7.____

    A. $2.85   B. $3.45   C. $3.95   D. $30.00   E. $30.95

8. It has been estimated that 125 kilowatt-hours of electricity are used each month in one average Housing Authority apartment at a cost of 14.8 cents per kilowatt-hour.
On this basis, the total cost of the electricity used in one year in a project containing 1,400 apartments is MOST NEARLY

8.____

    A. $20,000   B. $25,000   C. $200,000
    D. $250,000   E. $2,000,000

9. The walls and ceilings of 20 rooms are to be painted with the same kind of paint, each room being 15 feet long, 12 feet wide, and 10 feet high. Each room contains two windows, each 3 feet by 6 feet, and a door 3 feet by 8 feet, which are not to be painted. One gallon of paint covers 400 square feet of surface.
The number of gallons of paint needed is MOST NEARLY

9.____

    A. 33   B. 34   C. 35   D. 36   E. 75

10. A group of buildings is valued at $11,500,000. Assume that the cost of fire insurance for these buildings is 5.3 cents per $100 of valuation per year.
The cost of fire insurance for one year is MOST NEARLY

10.____

    A. $600   B. $6,000   C. $20,000
    D. $60,000   E. $2,000,000

11. Of the 15 employees in a certain unit, one-third earn $27,600 per year, three earn $32,600, one earns $46,400, and the rest earn $33,800.
The average salary of the employees of this unit is MOST NEARLY

11.____

    A. $31,000   B. $32,000   C. $33,000   D. $34,000   E. $35,000

12. Four pieces, each 2'5 3/8" long, are cut from a piece of pipe 16 1/2' long.
The length of the remaining piece of pipe is

12.____

    A. 6'8 1/2"   B. 6'10"   C. 6'10 3/8"
    D. 6'11 1/8"   E. 9'9 1/2"

13. A tenant earns E dollars a month, spends S dollars a week, and saves the rest.
The tenant's yearly savings can be expressed by

13.____

    A. 12(E-4S)   B. 12E - 52S   C. 12(E-S)
    D. 52(E-4S)   E. E - S

14. A unit of fifteen Housing Assistants has been assigned the job of interviewing applicants.   14.____
Each interview takes 35 minutes, and an additional 10 minutes is needed for making
entries and notes. The last interview each day is always scheduled so that it can be completed that day.
The number of applicants who can be interviewed in a week, consisting of five 7-hour
days, is MOST NEARLY

    A.   375   B.   525   C.   675   D.   700   E.   725

15. A review of the 14,000 applications for apartments in a certain project containing 1,200   15.____
apartments indicated that 4,800 applicants were eligible and 6,400 were ineligible. No
decision could be reached on the remaining applications because certain necessary
information was omitted by the applicants, but it was assumed that the proportion of eligible and ineligible applicants would remain the same as in those already decided.
On the basis of these figures, the percentage of eligible applicants who can be given
apartments in the project is

    A.   under 17%   B.   17%   C.   20%
    D.   25%   E.   33 1/3%

16. An oil burner in a housing development burns 76 gallons of fuel oil per hour. At 9 A.M. on   16.____
a very cold day, the superintendent asks the Housing Manager to put in an emergency
order for more fuel oil. At that time, he reports that he has on hand 266 gallons. At noon,
he again comes to the manager, notifying him that no oil has been delivered.
The MAXIMUM amount of time that he can continue to furnish heat without receiving
more oil is

    A.   no more time   B.   1/2 hour   C.   1 hour
    D.   1 1/2 hours   E.   2 hours

17. As a result of reports received by the Housing Authority concerning the reputed ineligibil-   17.____
ity of 756 tenants because of above-standard incomes, an intensive check of their
employers has been ordered. Four housing assistants have been assigned to this task.
At the end of 6 days at 7 hours each, they have checked on 336 tenants. In order to
speed up the investigation, two more housing assistants are assigned to this point.
If they worked at the same rate, the number of additional 7-hour days it would take to
complete the job is MOST NEARLY

    A.   1   B.   3   C.   5   D.   7   E.   9

18. A municipal aide on a special trip is returning to his office from a point 17 1/2 miles away,   18.____
and makes the return trip to his office at an average speed of 25 miles an hour, except for
a 15-minute stopover at one point to get a flat tire fixed.
The time it should take him to reach his office is MOST NEARLY _____ minutes.

    A.   12   B.   22   C.   36   D.   42   E.   57

19. A district office has an assigned staff of 320 employees. Of this number, 25% are not   19.____
available for duty due to illness, vacations, and other reasons. Of those who are available
for duty, 1/8 are assigned to auditing and special projects, and the rest to handling the
workload. The ACTUAL number of employees available for handling the workload is

    A.   350   B.   310   C.   270   D.   210   E.   180

20. Two dozen shuttlecocks and four badminton rackets are to be purchased for a play-   20.____
ground. The shuttlecocks are priced at $3.60 each, and the rackets at $27.50 each. The
playground receives a discount of 30% from these prices. The TOTAL cost of this equip-
ment is

   A. $72.90   B. $114.30   C. $13.7.48   D. $186.00   E. $220.70

21. On January 1, a family was receiving a public assistance allowance of $185 for food, $53   21.____
for clothing, $17.50 for utilities, and $22 for personal needs, all semi-monthly, and a
monthly allowance of $550 for rent. On May 1, the rent allowance was increased by 12%
but all other allowances remained the same for the rest of the year.
The TOTAL amount of money granted this family during the year was

   A. $10,528·   B. $13,262   C. $13,788
   D. $21,056   E. $27,676

22. It has been decided to make changes in food allotments to clients receiving public assis-   22.____
tance to conform to changes in food costs. Of the food allowance, 30% is intended for
meat, 30% for fruits and vegetables, 25% for groceries, and 15% for dairy products.
Assume that meat prices have gone up 10%, fruit and vegetable prices have gone down
20%, grocery prices have gone up 5%, and dairy prices have remained the same.
For a family that has been receiving $400 per month for food, the new monthly food
allowance will be

   A. $333   B. $375   C. $393   D. $403.50   E. $420

23. On January 1, a family was receiving a public assistance allowance of $195 for food, $63   23.____
for clothing, $27.50 for utilities, and $32 for personal needs, all semi-monthly, and a
monthly allowance of $510 for rent. On June 1, the rent allowance was increased by
12%, but all other allowances remained the same for the rest of the year.
The TOTAL amount of money granted this family during the year was

   A. $13,843.40   B. $14,107.20   C. $14,168.40
   D. $14,474.40   E. $16,886.80

24. A member of a family receiving public assistance amounting to $600 monthly has   24.____
obtained a part-time job, for which he is paid $40 a day. He is employed 3 days a week.
His carfare costs $3.00 per day and his lunches $2.00 per day. Assume that there are 4
1/3 weeks per month. The Department of Welfare requires that net earnings be deducted
from relief allowances.
The family's semi-monthly public assistance allowance should be reduced to

   A. $40.00   B. $72.50   C. $96.25   D. $123.75   E. $145.00

25. A couple living in a furnished room has been receiving a public assistance grant of $375   25.____
semi-monthly and has been paying a weekly rent of $75. The landlord has been granted
a 12% increase in rent. Assume that a month consists of 4 1/3 weeks.
The amount of the new semi-monthly grant, including this rent increase, that the couple will receive will be MOST NEARLY

   A. $394.50   B. $397   C. $409   D. $514   E. $557

KEY (CORRECT ANSWERS)

1.	D	11.	B
1.	C	12.	A
2.	C	13.	B
3.	A	14.	C
4.	B	15.	C
5.			
6.	D	16.	B
7.	B	17.	C
8.	D	18.	E
9.	A	19.	D
10.	B	20.	C

21.	C
22.	C
23.	C
24.	B
25.	A

———

SOLUTIONS TO PROBLEMS

1. For 3 months, income = $6250 + (.12)($7550) = $7156 Then, annual income = ($7154)(4) = $28,624, closest to $28,500

2. Maximum annual subsidy = ($8,000,000)(.0175) + (.01)($7,500,000) = $215,000

3. Cost in 2002 = $5589 / .046 = $121,500. The cost in 2003 = $121,500 + $5589 = $127,089. This means the cost in 2004 = ($127,089)(1.046) = $132,900

4. Average rate = total distance / total time = (25+25) ÷ (25/30 + 25/20) = 24 mph.

5. Out of 6000, number of eligible = 6000 - 2800 - 600 - 1200 - 400 = 1000. Thus, for 27,500 applications, (1/6)(27,500) = 4583 would be eligible. Finally, 1400 ÷ 4583 ≈ 30%

6. Number of applications in 2000 = (40,000)(1.05) = 42,000 Number of applications in 2001 = (42,000)(1.06) = 44,520 Then, (44,520-40,000) ÷ 40,000 = 11.3%

7. $28,500 ÷ [(75X110)] = $3.45 per sq.ft.

8. Total cost = (125)(.148)(12)(1400) = $310,800; closest to choice D of $250,000

9. Painted area of each room = (2)(15)(10) + (2)(12)(10) + (15)(12) - (2)(3)(6) - (3)(8) = 660 sq.ft. So, (20)(660) = 13,200 sq.ft. to be painted in all rooms. Finally, 13,200 / 400 = 33 gallons of paint needed

10. Insurance cost = (.053)($11,500,000)/$100 = $6095, closest to $6000

11. [(5)($27,600)+(3)($32,600)+(1)(46,400)+(6)($33,800)]/15 = $32,333, closest to $32,000

12. 16 1/2 - (4)(2'5 3/8") = 16'6" - 8'21 1/2" = 16'6" - 9'9 1/2" = 6'8 1/2"

13. Annual savings = 12E - 52S

14. $7 \div \dfrac{3}{4} = 9.\overline{3}$, which means each interviewer can interview a maximum of 9 applicants each day. Then, (5)(9)(15) = 675 applicants.

15. 4800/(4800+6400) = 3/7 eligible. On that assumption, there would be (3/7)(14,000) = 6000 eligible applicants. Then, 1200/6000 = 20%

16. 266 - (3)(76) = 38 gallons of oil left. Then, 38 / 76 =1/2 hour

17. (6)(7)(4) = 168 hrs. to check on 336 tenants. This means 2 tenants require 1 man-hour. Now, (6)(7)(x days) = man-hrs. would be needed to check the remaining 420 tenants. This requires 210 man-hours. So, (6)(7)(x) = 210. Solving, x = 5

18. $\dfrac{17.5}{25}$ = .7 hr. = 42 min. Total time = 42 + 15 = 57 min.

19. Number available = 320[1-.25-(1/8)(.75)] = 210

20. Total cost = (.70)[(24)($3.60)+(4)(27.50)] = $137.48

21. From January through April, amount = (8)($185+$53+$17,50+$22) + (4)($550) = $4420.
From May through December, amount = (16)($185+$53+$17.50+$22) + (8)($550)(1.12)
= $9368 Total annual amount = $4420 + $9368 = $13,788

22. Meat allowance = ($400)(.30)(1.10) = $132; fruit and vegetable allowance =
($400)(.30)(.80) = $96; grocery allowance = ($400)(.25)(1.05) = $105; dairy allowance =
($400)(,15) = $60 New monthly allowance = $132 + $96 + $105 + $.60 = $393

23. From January through May, amount = (10)($195+$63+$27.50+$32) + (5)($510) = $5725.
From June through December, amount = (14)($195+$63+$27.50+$32) + (7)($510)(1.12)
= $8443.40. Total annual amount = $5725 + $8443.40 = $14,168.40

24. Monthly assistance should be reduced to $600 - [(40)(3)(4 1/3) - ($5)(3)(4 1/3)] = $145.
So, the semi-monthly amount is now $145 / 2 = $72.50

25. ($75) (4 1/3) / 2 = $162.50 = original semi-monthly rent.
New semi-monthly rent = (162.50)(1.12) = $182. Since this represents an increase of
$19.50, the new semi-monthly grant will be increased to $375 + $19.50 = $394.50

———

ANSWER SHEET

TEST NO. _____ PART _____ TITLE OF POSITION _____

(AS GIVEN IN EXAMINATION ANNOUNCEMENT - INCLUDE OPTION, IF ANY)

PLACE OF EXAMINATION _____ DATE _____
(CITY OR TOWN)   (STATE)

RATING

USE THE SPECIAL PENCIL.   MAKE GLOSSY BLACK MARKS.

	A B C D E		A B C D E		A B C D E		A B C D E		A B C D E
1	:: :: :: :: ::	26	:: :: :: :: ::	51	:: :: :: :: ::	76	:: :: :: :: ::	101	:: :: :: :: ::
2	:: :: :: :: ::	27	:: :: :: :: ::	52	:: :: :: :: ::	77	:: :: :: :: ::	102	:: :: :: :: ::
3	:: :: :: :: ::	28	:: :: :: :: ::	53	:: :: :: :: ::	78	:: :: :: :: ::	103	:: :: :: :: ::
4	:: :: :: :: ::	29	:: :: :: :: ::	54	:: :: :: :: ::	79	:: :: :: :: ::	104	:: :: :: :: ::
5	:: :: :: :: ::	30	:: :: :: :: ::	55	:: :: :: :: ::	80	:: :: :: :: ::	105	:: :: :: :: ::
6	:: :: :: :: ::	31	:: :: :: :: ::	56	:: :: :: :: ::	81	:: :: :: :: ::	106	:: :: :: :: ::
7	:: :: :: :: ::	32	:: :: :: :: ::	57	:: :: :: :: ::	82	:: :: :: :: ::	107	:: :: :: :: ::
8	:: :: :: :: ::	33	:: :: :: :: ::	58	:: :: :: :: ::	83	:: :: :: :: ::	108	:: :: :: :: ::
9	:: :: :: :: ::	34	:: :: :: :: ::	59	:: :: :: :: ::	84	:: :: :: :: ::	109	:: :: :: :: ::
10	:: :: :: :: ::	35	:: :: :: :: ::	60	:: :: :: :: ::	85	:: :: :: :: ::	110	:: :: :: :: ::

Make only ONE mark for each answer.   Additional and stray marks may be
counted as mistakes.   In making corrections, erase errors COMPLETELY.

	A B C D E		A B C D E		A B C D E		A B C D E		A B C D E
11	:: :: :: :: ::	36	:: :: :: :: ::	61	:: :: :: :: ::	86	:: :: :: :: ::	111	:: :: :: :: ::
12	:: :: :: :: ::	37	:: :: :: :: ::	62	:: :: :: :: ::	87	:: :: :: :: ::	112	:: :: :: :: ::
13	:: :: :: :: ::	38	:: :: :: :: ::	63	:: :: :: :: ::	88	:: :: :: :: ::	113	:: :: :: :: ::
14	:: :: :: :: ::	39	:: :: :: :: ::	64	:: :: :: :: ::	89	:: :: :: :: ::	114	:: :: :: :: ::
15	:: :: :: :: ::	40	:: :: :: :: ::	65	:: :: :: :: ::	90	:: :: :: :: ::	115	:: :: :: :: ::
16	:: :: :: :: ::	41	:: :: :: :: ::	66	:: :: :: :: ::	91	:: :: :: :: ::	116	:: :: :: :: ::
17	:: :: :: :: ::	42	:: :: :: :: ::	67	:: :: :: :: ::	92	:: :: :: :: ::	117	:: :: :: :: ::
18	:: :: :: :: ::	43	:: :: :: :: ::	68	:: :: :: :: ::	93	:: :: :: :: ::	118	:: :: :: :: ::
19	:: :: :: :: ::	44	:: :: :: :: ::	69	:: :: :: :: ::	94	:: :: :: :: ::	119	:: :: :: :: ::
20	:: :: :: :: ::	45	:: :: :: :: ::	70	:: :: :: :: ::	95	:: :: :: :: ::	120	:: :: :: :: ::
21	:: :: :: :: ::	46	:: :: :: :: ::	71	:: :: :: :: ::	96	:: :: :: :: ::	121	:: :: :: :: ::
22	:: :: :: :: ::	47	:: :: :: :: ::	72	:: :: :: :: ::	97	:: :: :: :: ::	122	:: :: :: :: ::
23	:: :: :: :: ::	48	:: :: :: :: ::	73	:: :: :: :: ::	98	:: :: :: :: ::	123	:: :: :: :: ::
24	:: :: :: :: ::	49	:: :: :: :: ::	74	:: :: :: :: ::	99	:: :: :: :: ::	124	:: :: :: :: ::
25	:: :: :: :: ::	50	:: :: :: :: ::	75	:: :: :: :: ::	100	:: :: :: :: ::	125	:: :: :: :: ::

ANSWER SHEET

TEST NO. _____ PART _____ TITLE OF POSITION _____

(AS GIVEN IN EXAMINATION ANNOUNCEMENT - INCLUDE OPTION, IF ANY)

PLACE OF EXAMINATION _____ DATE _____

(CITY OR TOWN)　　　　　(STATE)

WITHDRAWN

RATING

USE THE SPECIAL PENCIL.　MAKE GLOSSY BLACK MARKS.

#	A B C D E	#	A B C D E	#	A B C D E	#	A B C D E	#	A B C D E
1	:: :: :: :: ::	26	:: :: :: :: ::	51	:: :: :: :: ::	76	:: :: :: :: ::	101	:: :: :: :: ::
2	:: :: :: :: ::	27	:: :: :: :: ::	52	:: :: :: :: ::	77	:: :: :: :: ::	102	:: :: :: :: ::
3	:: :: :: :: ::	28	:: :: :: :: ::	53	:: :: :: :: ::	78	:: :: :: :: ::	103	:: :: :: :: ::
4	:: :: :: :: ::	29	:: :: :: :: ::	54	:: :: :: :: ::	79	:: :: :: :: ::	104	:: :: :: :: ::
5	:: :: :: :: ::	30	:: :: :: :: ::	55	:: :: :: :: ::	80	:: :: :: :: ::	105	:: :: :: :: ::
6	:: :: :: :: ::	31	:: :: :: :: ::	56	:: :: :: :: ::	81	:: :: :: :: ::	106	:: :: :: :: ::
7	:: :: :: :: ::	32	:: :: :: :: ::	57	:: :: :: :: ::	82	:: :: :: :: ::	107	:: :: :: :: ::
8	:: :: :: :: ::	33	:: :: :: :: ::	58	:: :: :: :: ::	83	:: :: :: :: ::	108	:: :: :: :: ::
9	:: :: :: :: ::	34	:: :: :: :: ::	59	:: :: :: :: ::	84	:: :: :: :: ::	109	:: :: :: :: ::
10	:: :: :: :: ::	35	:: :: :: :: ::	60	:: :: :: :: ::	85	:: :: :: :: ::	110	:: :: :: :: ::

Make only ONE mark for each answer.　Additional and stray marks may be
counted as mistakes.　In making corrections, erase errors COMPLETELY.

#	A B C D E	#	A B C D E	#	A B C D E	#	A B C D E	#	A B C D E
11	:: :: :: :: ::	36	:: :: :: :: ::	61	:: :: :: :: ::	86	:: :: :: :: ::	111	:: :: :: :: ::
12	:: :: :: :: ::	37	:: :: :: :: ::	62	:: :: :: :: ::	87	:: :: :: :: ::	112	:: :: :: :: ::
13	:: :: :: :: ::	38	:: :: :: :: ::	63	:: :: :: :: ::	88	:: :: :: :: ::	113	:: :: :: :: ::
14	:: :: :: :: ::	39	:: :: :: :: ::	64	:: :: :: :: ::	89	:: :: :: :: ::	114	:: :: :: :: ::
15	:: :: :: :: ::	40	:: :: :: :: ::	65	:: :: :: :: ::	90	:: :: :: :: ::	115	:: :: :: :: ::
16	:: :: :: :: ::	41	:: :: :: :: ::	66	:: :: :: :: ::	91	:: :: :: :: ::	116	:: :: :: :: ::
17	:: :: :: :: ::	42	:: :: :: :: ::	67	:: :: :: :: ::	92	:: :: :: :: ::	117	:: :: :: :: ::
18	:: :: :: :: ::	43	:: :: :: :: ::	68	:: :: :: :: ::	93	:: :: :: :: ::	118	:: :: :: :: ::
19	:: :: :: :: ::	44	:: :: :: :: ::	69	:: :: :: :: ::	94	:: :: :: :: ::	119	:: :: :: :: ::
20	:: :: :: :: ::	45	:: :: :: :: ::	70	:: :: :: :: ::	95	:: :: :: :: ::	120	:: :: :: :: ::
21	:: :: :: :: ::	46	:: :: :: :: ::	71	:: :: :: :: ::	96	:: :: :: :: ::	121	:: :: :: :: ::
22	:: :: :: :: ::	47	:: :: :: :: ::	72	:: :: :: :: ::	97	:: :: :: :: ::	122	:: :: :: :: ::
23	:: :: :: :: ::	48	:: :: :: :: ::	73	:: :: :: :: ::	98	:: :: :: :: ::	123	:: :: :: :: ::
24	:: :: :: :: ::	49	:: :: :: :: ::	74	:: :: :: :: ::	99	:: :: :: :: ::	124	:: :: :: :: ::
25	:: :: :: :: ::	50	:: :: :: :: ::	75	:: :: :: :: ::	100	:: :: :: :: ::	125	:: :: :: :: ::